Out of the Air

Longman Imprint Books
General Editor: Michael Marland CBE

Companion cassettes, with readings of some of the key stories, are available for the following:
The Leaping Lad and other stories
The Human Element
A Sillitoe Selection
Late Night on Watling Street
A Casual Acquaintance
Loves, Hopes, and Fears
A John Wain Selection

LONGMAN IMPRINT BOOKS

Out of the Air

Five plays for radio
by
Stan Barstow
Don Haworth
David Campton
Ken Whitmore
Ivor Wilson

selected and edited by
Alfred Bradley

Senior Drama Producer
BBC North

questions for discussion and suggestions for writing by
Chris Buckton
Islington Green School, London

Longman

LONGMAN GROUP LIMITED
London

*Associated companies branches and representatives
throughout the world*

This edition © Longman Group Ltd 1978
This edition first published 1978

ISBN 0 582 23356 9

Printed in Hong Kong by
Bright Sun Printing Press Co. Ltd.

We are grateful to the following for permission to include these
plays which are in copyright:

The authors and the authors' agent Harvey Unna & Stephen
Durbridge Ltd, 14 Beaumont Mews, Marylebone High Street,
London W1, for *We Could Always Fit a Sidecar* by Stan Barstow,
There's No Point in Arguing the Toss by Don Haworth and *Jump!*
by Ken Whitmore; Evans Plays, Montague House, Russell
Square, London WC1, the author and the author's agent, Actac
Ltd, 16 Cadogan Lane, London SW1 for *Relics* by David
Campton; the author and author's agent, Margery Vosper Ltd,
Suite 8, 26 Charing Cross Road, London WC2, for *Take Any Day*
by Ivor Wilson; Blackie and Son Ltd. for an essay (slightly
adapted) by Michael Marland, from *Worth a Hearing*.

All applications for performance rights should be addressed to the
agents in each case as above.

Contents

Out of the Air
an introductory note

In spite of the attractions of television and the theatre, radio drama still has a strong appeal for millions of listeners who prefer plays which are partly created within their own heads. Nearly six hundred plays are broadcast by the BBC each year, many of them written specially for the medium: there is no doubt that the economy of radio gives it a great advantage over other forms of drama production and consequently it is able to offer opportunities for experiment which television and the theatre, burdened with enormous production costs, can rarely afford.

The five plays included in this volume have been chosen for their strong contrasts in style and content and because they provide opportunities for a group of actors to play a wide range of parts. *We Could Always Fit a Sidecar* deals with two lonely people and a broken engagement; *There's No Point in Arguing the Toss* is a hilarious account of two brothers who are determined to take their dad home on the bus as they do after every Saturday outing—even though he has just died of a heart attack; *Relics* is a study of women corroded by greed; *Jump!* tells a story about a boy trying to persuade everybody in the world to work together; and *Take Any Day* shows us some of the strains of modern life as they affect an overworked doctor practising in a bleak industrial area.

The texts are almost identical with the original radio scripts, but the studio directions have been simplified so that they can be read in the classroom. At the same time the sound effects are easily picked out if you decide to go a step further and record a full-scale radio production. Despite the complex and expensive equipment used in professional broadcasting studios, a great deal can be achieved using a school tape recorder, and with patience and ingenuity it should be possible to create all of the effects in the plays without difficulty. Detailed suggestions for the setting up of a simple studio and notes on radio production are given in Producing Radio Plays in Schools at the end of the book.

We Could Always Fit A Sidecar

Stan Barstow

The Cast

Foreman

Harry

First Mechanic

Second Mechanic

Shop Assistant

Mrs Baynes

Thelma Baynes

Jack Baynes

Delivery Man

Postman

Mrs Kitson

We Could Always Fit A Sidecar

Most of us experience loneliness at some time in our lives. Some people, like Harry, who are shy and retiring by nature, learn to live with it and resent people who try to impose friendship on them.

Harry is a good mechanic but although respected for his conscientious workmanship, doesn't find it easy to mix with other people and consequently gets teased by his mates. His motor-bike, on which he lavishes most of his spare time, has become the most important thing in his life.

Needing to live near the factory, Harry finds a bed-sitting room in the Baynes's house where he leads a quiet life and is answerable to nobody. Thelma, the Baynes's daughter, is a warmhearted, cheerful girl who hasn't any ambition apart from finding the right man to marry. Thelma and Harry are thrown together when Mrs Baynes decides to drag her family to a picnic; Harry has no desire to join the outing but is forced to go in order to protect his radio, which Mr Baynes insists on borrowing so that he can follow the test match.

Thelma and Harry go off together to return the tea jug to a farm and on their way back Thelma falls into the river. By the time Harry, who has never touched a girl in his life, has pulled her out of the water, he finds himself letting slip words of love, which he later regrets and Thelma's head is filled with wedding bells.

Harry is trapped but decides to make the best of it. He finds a small house and with Thelma's help begins to make it into a little palace. He is angry and upset when she loses her engagement ring through an act of carelessness and Thelma hits back by accusing him of being more interested in possessions than in other people.

After they have parted, Harry tries to live in the house alone but, although it may be comfortable, it is as cheerless as a furniture shop window: he finds that he is lonelier than ever and that he needs Thelma as much as she needs him.

Fade in.

A motor repair shop
A power drill in the foreground.

FOREMAN It's eight o'clock, Harry. (*no reply*) Harry!

HARRY What?

FOREMAN It's time to knock off.

HARRY Aye, all right.

The power drill whines to a stop. Cross fade to:

The locker room
The sound of running water. A locker door opens and shuts.

FIRST MECH. Well, that's another spot of overtime in the bag.

SECOND MECH. Aye. It'll help pay for the booze and crumpet over the weekend.

The door opens. Harry enters.

FIRST MECH. Here, you can use this basin, Harry. I've finished.

HARRY Ta.

FIRST MECH. Coming on the town with us tomorrow night, then, Harry?

HARRY I don't think so.

FIRST MECH. Do you good to let yourself go once in a while, y'know.

HARRY Oh, I'm all right.

SECOND MECH. What do *you* work overtime for, Harry?

HARRY Same reason as you do.

FIRST MECH. Aye, time and a half.

SECOND MECH. I don't know what you do with your brass. You must be worth a mint.

FIRST MECH. He spends it on his hobbies, don't you, Harry?

SECOND MECH. Aye, so do I. Best hobby there is.

FIRST MECH. Oh, Harry's all right. He's got a bit laid on at home. Haven't you, Harry?

SECOND MECH. Who's that, then?

FIRST MECH. His landlady's daughter, Thelma.

SECOND MECH. All right is she?

FIRST MECH. Just like them big busty women in old paintings. You wouldn't know where to take hold first. (*laughs*)

SECOND MECH. Is she included in the board and lodgings, then?

FIRST MECH. No, she's one of the extras.

HARRY I'll be off, then.

FIRST MECH. Aye, see you Monday, Harry.

The door opens.

FOREMAN (*approaching*) Just off, are you, Harry?

HARRY Aye. So long. (*he goes*)

FOREMAN So long. Have a nice weekend.

FIRST MECH. (*calls*) And don't get into any trouble.

(*laughs*) That'll be the day.

FOREMAN Have you two been pulling Harry's leg again?

FIRST MECH. Aw, he's like a soft old sheep. You can't help having a go at him.

FOREMAN He's the best mechanic I've seen in some time. I wish there were a few more that did as much work, instead o' gabbin' so much.

FIRST MECH. Now we know where *we* stand, Jeff.

SECOND MECH. Aye. You can't get a good word out of anybody these days. (*changing the subject*) Is old Harry really doing a bit for his land-lady's daughter?

FIRST MECH. It'll surprise me if he is. He's a right bachelor is that one. Catch *him* spending his brass on women.

SECOND MECH. It takes all sorts. . . .

FIRST MECH. Mind your own business, and get value for money. That's Harry, me old love.

Fade out.

Fade in.

A shoeshop.

The bell rings as the street door opens.

WOMAN ASS'T. (*approaching*) Can I help you?

HARRY I left a fifty pence deposit on a pair of shoes. Thursday it was.

WOMAN ASS'T Oh yes, I remember. Mr—er. . . .

HARRY West.

ASSISTANT Yes. Let me see. I put them. . . . Yes, here they are. (*she opens the shoebox*) Those the ones?

HARRY Yes.

ASSISTANT You did try them on when you were in?

HARRY Yes. (*pause*) I'm just wondering now, seeing 'em again. You don't think they're a bit on the flashy side, do you?

ASSISTANT Flashy? These? Not a bit. These two-tones are all the go just now.

HARRY I mean for somebody like me. My age.

ASSISTANT You're only a young man. Somebody middle-aged, perhaps I'd say otherwise, but not you.

HARRY You've a nice pair of plain tan in the window.

ASSISTANT Well, it's up to you, of course. But this is the last pair of these in your size. If you don't take 'em they'll be snapped up before the morning's out.

HARRY Aye. (*pause*) All right, then.

5

ASSISTANT You'll have them?

HARRY Yes.

ASSISTANT I'm sure you'll be highly delighted when you've worn them once. (*she wraps them up*) Let me see, fifty pence deposit. That leaves just five ninety-nine to pay.
Fade out.

Fade in.

The Baynes's House.

A test match on television. We hear the voice of the commentator, the click of bat on ball, distant applause. England are struggling just before lunch on the third day.

MRS BAYNES (*approaching*) Is the table ready, Thelma?

THELMA All about.

MRS BAYNES Right. We can start then. Come and get your dinner, Jack.

JACK (*absently*) Aye...

MRS BAYNES I'll just give Harry a shout. (*she goes off and calls up the stairs*) Harry! Dinner's ready.

HARRY (*distant*) Right!

MRS BAYNES (*approaching*) Jack, I said your dinner's on t'table.

JACK Aye. (*groans*) Oh! Dammit man, watch what you're doing. Oh, we're going to lose this if they don't buckle to.

MRS BAYNES You'll lose more than a cricket match if you don't come and get your dinner.
(*she switches the set off*)

JACK Here, there's ten minutes left before lunch!

MRS BAYNES *Your* lunch is ready now, and if you think I'm going to spend half the morning in the kitchen getting it ready only to watch you let it go cold, you've another think coming. What with you and your sport, and him upstairs and his motor-bike...

JACK He hasn't got his motor-bike upstairs, has he?

MRS BAYNES Who?

JACK Harry.

MRS BAYNES 'Course he hasn't got his motor-bike upstairs. What're you talking about?

JACK You said "him upstairs and his motor-bike."

MRS BAYNES What if I did? I didn't mean he'd got his bike upstairs.

JACK Well, if he hasn't got his motor-bike upstairs it can't be that 'at's stopping him coming down for his dinner, can it?

MRS BAYNES Are you trying to addle my brains, or what?

JACK Nay, all I said was...

6

MRS BAYNES Oh, get your dinner an' let your meat stop your mouth. (*she goes away and calls again*) Harry! Your dinner's on the table. *Fade out.*

Fade in.

Thelma and Mrs Baynes are washing up.

MRS BAYNES Is that the last of the pots?

THELMA Yeh, that's the lot.

MRS BAYNES Give us 'em here, then.

THELMA We could go up into the park and take some tea with us. That'd be nice. You see all sorts of people in the park.

MRS BAYNES I've got an urge to get right out of town this afternoon. I thought we might try Craddle Woods.

THELMA Ooh, that'd be lovely. We could be there in half an hour on the bus. Only trouble is me dad.

MRS BAYNES What about your dad?

THELMA We'll never drag him away from the Test Match.

MRS BAYNES Your dad's going on a picnic with us this afternoon and there's no argument about it.

THELMA (*at the window*) Look, there's Lottie Sharpe going down the yard. All dressed up. She's off to meet her fiance, I expect. Look at her shoes. I don't know how she can walk in 'em. Don't they set her legs off lovely?

MRS BAYNES Spindle-shanks.

THELMA Nay they're not, Mother. She's got lovely legs. In fact, I think she's smashing looking altogether. I wish I looked like her.

MRS BAYNES Don't talk so silly. A fine well-set-up young woman like you.

THELMA I wonder what she feels like, getting married next month.

MRS BAYNES You'll know soon enough, when it's your turn.

THELMA Me? I haven't even got a chap.

MRS BAYNES You will have one o' these days, when Mister Right turns up.

THELMA So you keep saying.

MRS BAYNES Well, there's Harry, for instance. He's single and respectable, with a good head on his shoulders.

THELMA Harry! I don't think he's ever noticed me. I bet he doesn't know what I look like. That motor bike's all he thinks about. An' anyway, p'raps he's not my type.

MRS BAYNES There's plenty more men in the world. (*sharply*) But you'll have to wake up a bit to catch one. Don't rub all the pattern off that plate. Let's get finished or we'll be stuck here all afternoon.

THELMA I'd better go and see if I can talk me dad round.

MRS BAYNES *(calling after her)* Aye, tell him to be getting himself ready.
Fade out.

Fade in.

Jack Baynes is snoring in the chair.

THELMA Dad. *(no response)* Dad. Are you asleep?

JACK *(spluttering awake)* What? What's up now? Can't a feller have a minutes peace?

THELMA Me mam and me want to go on a picnic to Craddle Woods.

JACK Aye, righto. *(he settles down again)*

THELMA And me mam says it's time you were getting ready.

JACK Me? I'm not going on no picnic. I'm watching t'Test Match.

MRS BAYNES *(approaching)* We're going on a picnic and you're coming with us. It's a crying shame to waste such a grand afternoon.

JACK I'm not wasting it. I'm watching t'Test Match.

MRS BAYNES Come on and stir yourself, or we shall never get off. You can hear about the Test Match on the News tonight.

JACK I'm watching it on the telly this afternoon, and that's final.

THELMA *(plaintive)* Oh Dad!

JACK You and your mother get your way on most things, but I won't have you interfering with my cricket.

MRS BAYNES Harry's got that portable radio of his, Thelma. If we had that your dad could come with us and listen to the match as well.

THELMA D'you think he'd lend it to us? You know how he is with his things. He hardly lets anybody touch anything of his.

MRS BAYNES We can ask for nowt.

THELMA Dad, will you come if we take Harry's radio with us?

JACK If the pair of you aren't enough to pester a feller to death. . . .

MRS BAYNES Where is Harry now? He hasn't gone out, has he?

THELMA He's in the yard, I think; playing with his motor-bike.

MRS BAYNES Go and ask him, Thelma. See what he says.

THELMA Yes, I will.

MRS BAYNES *(calling after her)* Oh, and I say. Ask him if he'd like to come with us. The more the merrier, eh?
Fade out.

Fade in.

The back yard.
Harry revs the engine of his bike then lets it tick over.

THELMA Hello.

HARRY Oh, hello.

THELMA Are you busy?

HARRY You're *allus* busy with a motor-bike, if you look after it properly.

THELMA What are you doing now, then?

HARRY Oh, just checking the timing, and things.

THELMA (*not consciously trying to flatter*) You must be clever to know all about motor-bikes and cars and things.

HARRY Oh, you get the hang of 'em y'know.

THELMA Me mam and me want to go on a picnic this afternoon.

HARRY Oh, yes?

THELMA Only me dad won't go 'cos he wants to watch the Test Match on the telly.

HARRY Ah!

THELMA We was wondering if you'd like to lend us that portable radio of yours. If we had that me dad could come with us and hear the match as well.
(*the engine stops*)

HARRY (*he doesn't want to lend the radio but doesn't know how to refuse*) Well, I, er. . . . I dunno. You see. . . .

THELMA You know how stubborn me dad is about his cricket. And me mam won't go without him. (*no response*) We're going to Craddle Woods. It'll be lovely there today. Why don't you come with us, then you can look after the radio yourself?

HARRY Well I reckon I'd have to. Only, I'd summat else in mind, really. There's jobs to do on the bike.

THELMA I don't know how you can mend cars all week and then work on your bike at weekends.

HARRY Oh, but this is me own. That makes a difference. Besides, you've got to keep up to things, else you're soon in trouble.

THELMA But it can wait, can't it? It's such a lovely day, and if me dad can't hear his cricket we shan't be able to go. It's going to spoil it for everybody. If you'd let us take it we'd look after it. We really would take care of it.

HARRY Oh, no. I couldn't do that.

THELMA You mean, you'll come, then? Oh, I am glad. We can have a lovely time.

HARRY (*He's trapped but he's all for an easy life*) When are you setting off?

THELMA In about half an hour, I should think. (*going*) Thanks ever so much, Harry. I'll tell 'em to be getting ready.

HARRY (*to himself*) Now how the hell did I come to drop in for that? *Fade out.*

Fade in.

In the woods.

MRS BAYNES Here we are, then. This'll do nicely. (*she sits down, gasping a little*) Isn't it warm, though?

JACK Where's Thelma and Harry?

MRS BAYNES They called at that farm to see if we could have a jug of tea. We really ought to buy a thermos flask, y'know, then we could take drinks with us.

JACK Take 'em where?

MRS BAYNES On picnics and outings, like this.

JACK We're not making a reg'lar thing o' this, I can tell you. Saturday afternoon's my sports time. It allus has been. (*testily*) Where the heck's Harry with that wireless?

MRS BAYNES What do you make of Harry, Jack?

JACK How d'you mean?

MRS BAYNES I mean, what do you think about him?

JACK I don't know 'at I've ever thought about it.

MRS BAYNES Well, he's been with us six months and above now. You must have an opinion. Do you think he likes our Thelma, for instance?

JACK Now how should I know that? Harry's like all the rest of us, if you ask me—all right if he's left alone.

MRS BAYNES Oh, you... You talk as if men wanted nowt but to be hermits.

JACK Now there's a thought...

THELMA (*approaching*) Ooh, this is a lovely place. Look, you can see 'em playing golf right over there.

HARRY Hockey at the halt.

THELMA What?

HARRY Hockey at the halt. It's what we used to call golf when we were kids.

THELMA (*unsmiling*) Oh, I see.

MRS BAYNES Do they make tea, then, Thelma?

THELMA Yes. We can have a jug when we're ready.

JACK Let's have your wireless, then, Harry. They'll be commentating again now. (*pause*) Where's your Radio 3, then?

HARRY Should be there somewhere.

JACK There's nowt coming through.

MRS BAYNES Y'know, we should come here more often, 'stead o' sticking in that mucky town. Me and your father used to come here courting. Didn't we, Dad?

JACK (*preoccupied*) Hmmmm?

MRS BAYNES I hope you're not going to have your head stuck inside that thing all afternoon. If that's all you can find to do you might as well have stopped at home.

JACK That's what I wanted to do. What's up with the flaming thing? I can't get no reception.

HARRY (*hastily*) Here, don't shake it. Let me...It might be all these trees.

JACK There's nowt coming through at all. If you ask me it's broken.

HARRY It was playing all right before we came out.

JACK Well, it's not playing now.

MRS BAYNES Here we are, next to nature, and all they can do is fiddle with a wireless set!

JACK Is your valves in right? Happen there's one worked loose in its socket.

HARRY It doesn't work on valves. It's a transistor.

JACK Well let's have t'back off an' see what's wrong.
Fade out.

Fade in.
Some time later.

JACK Stuck here in t'middle o' this flaming wilderness and no idea what's going on.

MRS BAYNES I wish you'd shut up about that daft cricket match.

JACK I never wanted to come in the first place, but you can't leave people in peace.

MRS BAYNES It makes a nice little party with the four of us.

JACK It isn't as if there's owt to do when you get here.

MRS BAYNES You can sit and enjoy the fresh air. Everybody else is enjoying it, so why can't you? You're enjoying it, aren't you, Harry?

HARRY What? Oh, yeh.

THELMA Can't you put wireless batteries in a hot oven to bring 'em back to life?

JACK We never thought to bring a hot oven with us, though, did we?

HARRY I think I can see the connection that's split. It needs a spot of solder.

JACK We haven't got a soldering iron, either.

MRS BAYNES Is there any tea left in that jug, Thelma?

THELMA No, it's empty. I think I'll take it back to the farm.

HARRY Here, I'll take it, if you like. I wouldn't mind a walk.

MRS BAYNES Why don't you both go?

HARRY Well, I....

THELMA Yeh, come on, Harry. Leave me mam and dad on their own. They might want to do a bit of courting.

MRS BAYNES That's likely, that is! You two get off for ten minutes, if you want. (*coyly*) And behave yourselves, won't you?
Fade out.

Fade in.

Another part of the woods.

THELMA Ooh, it's better here under the trees. That farmyard, it was boiling.

HARRY Yeh. I wouldn't fancy being a sheep, this weather.

THELMA I wish we were at the seaside. I'd love to go in the sea just now. Trouble is, when you are there it's usually either cold or raining. We had a week last year at Bridlington and it rained every day.

HARRY Yeh, it can be a bit chancy at Bridlington.

THELMA I like Scarborough better, but me mam can't stand all the hills. Where do you like, Harry?

HARRY I dunno, really.

THELMA Didn't you have seaside holidays when you were a little lad?

HARRY I went with the cubs once. And I stopped with me auntie at Morecambe for a bit.

THELMA Ooh, fancy living at the seaside. That must be lovely.

HARRY Aw, you get used to it, like owt else.

THELMA Still, it's lovely having a place where you can go when you like.

HARRY I don't go any more. Me auntie's dead.

THELMA Was she your only relative?

HARRY As far as I know. . . . Look, there's the beck, you can have a paddle if you want to cool off.

THELMA What about you?

HARRY Naw, it's nowt in my line.

THELMA You'll wait for me, though, won't you?

HARRY Yeh, go on, I'll wait.
Thelma goes into the water.

THELMA Ooh, it's lovely and cool. You want to come in.

HARRY Is it deep?

THELMA Yeh, up to the knees. Look.

HARRY Watch out for the crabs.

THELMA It's better when you make waves.

HARRY I should watch out. You never know. . . .

THELMA Oh, I've trodden on something. I can't keep up!
A splash as she falls in the water.
(*cries out*) Harry! Help me!

HARRY Bloody hell!

Another splash as Harry wades in and rescues her.

THELMA (*gasping a little*) Gosh, I thought I was going in over me head.

HARRY You're all right now.

THELMA I'm soaked through, though. You'd better put me down. I'm wetting your shirt.

HARRY (*holding Thelma has roused sexual excitement in him and he doesn't want to put her down*) That's all right.

THELMA I'm heavy though, aren't I? Aren't I too heavy?

HARRY You're no weight at all.

THELMA Now you're joking. They don't call me Lottie Sharp—seven stone wet through. (*she giggles a little uncertainly*) Come on, Harry. We can't stop like this all afternoon.
He lets her down.
Thanks. It's a good job you were here or I'd have gone right under.

HARRY Your foot's bleeding.

THELMA I trod on something on the bottom. A broken bottle, I think. That's why I lost me balance.

HARRY Sit down and I'll wrap me hankie round it.

THELMA (*shivers*) Ugh! I've cooled off now, all right. Just look at this frock.

HARRY It'll soon dry in the sun.

THELMA Aye, but in the meantime I feel like one of them women in telly commercials. Them that come out of the water showing all they've got.

HARRY You've got a good figure.

THELMA Go on!

HARRY I mean it.

THELMA What brought all this on?

HARRY I don't know what you mean.

THELMA You've never taken a blind bit o' notice of me before.

HARRY How do you know?

THELMA Why didn't you say something, then?

HARRY Well, I. . . .

THELMA Was it because you're shy? (*softly, half embarrassed*) There's no need to be shy with me, you big daft lump.

HARRY Who're you calling a big daft lump?

THELMA You, for being shy with me. (*he embraces her*) Steady on, you'll get your shirt all wet again.

HARRY I don't care. Give us a kiss.
They kiss.

THELMA Mmmm. (*softly*) Shall I tell you something?

HARRY What?

THELMA When you got hold of me and lifted me out of the water. Just picked me up and whisked me out, I felt all safe and.... well, as though I was looked after.

HARRY (*he is now beyond caution*) I like looking after you. I'd like to look after you all along.

THELMA Would you, Harry? All along? (*they kiss again*) Mmm, that's nice. (*a pause*) No, Harry, we mustn't. Not now. Somebody might come, and me mam'll be wondering where we are. Oh! Just look at your new shoes! They're sopping. And your trousers are wet through to the knees.

HARRY They'll be all right.

THELMA I'll press your trousers for you when we get home. Oh! Isn't it funny how things happen? I never expected anything like this happening when we set off. Did you? You think nothin's happening at all, then all of a sudden something does.
Fade out.

Fade in.

MRS BAYNES I don't know where they can have got to. They've been away long enough to take six jugs back.

JACK They're old enough to look after themselves.

MRS BAYNES Is that them coming now? Yes it is. (*calls*) Now then, what have you two been up to? (*as she sees*) Why, Thelma, you're....

THELMA Ooh, it was ever so funny, Mam. I went paddling in the beck and cut me foot on a bit of glass. I'd have gone right under, but Harry fished me out and wrapped me foot up in his hankie.

MRS BAYNES You're soaked to the skin, lass.

THELMA I know I am. But guess what, Mam. You'll never guess.

MRS BAYNES What won't I guess?

THELMA Me and Harry's engaged!

MRS BAYNES Well!
A pause.

JACK You didn't meet anybody to tell you the cricket score, did you?
Fade out.

Fade in.

The Baynes's house.

MRS BAYNES Richards did the catering when your cousin Alice got married. And they were very good when we buried your grandfather.

THELMA Lottie's having Deardens, and a reception in the Drill Hall.

There'll be sixty-five people sitting down, she says.

MRS BAYNES Reason in all things, I allus say. You'd think some folk were Royalty, the show they put on. Where's Harry?

THELMA Up in his room, I expect.

MRS BAYNES You'd think he'd want to be down here, talking to his fiance.

THELMA He's p'raps feeling a bit shy. I'll ask him down when I take him his trousers.

Jack puts his newspaper aside impatiently.

JACK (*fed up*) You wouldn't believe it. Rain stopped play. I can't understand it. We haven't had a drop all day.

THELMA (*dreamily*) No, it's been a lovely day.

Fade out.

Fade in.

Harry's room.

HARRY (*to himself, gloomily*) Ruined. . . .

A knock. The door opens slightly.

THELMA Can I come in?

HARRY Yeh, come in.

THELMA There, I've pressed your trousers. They're as good as new again now.

HARRY Oh, right, thanks.

THELMA Are you trying to polish your new shoes?

HARRY Yeh, yeh, I am.

THELMA They'll p'raps shine up when they've had a real chance to dry.

HARRY Yeh.

THELMA I'll put your trousers over this chair. You'd better let them air before you wear them again.

HARRY Okay. Thanks.

THELMA It's a shame about your wireless. I hope it'll repair.

HARRY I expect it will.

THELMA Ooh, I've never seen this before. I didn't know you liked trains.

HARRY It's a locomotive.

THELMA Well, locomotive. Did you make it yourself?

HARRY Yeh, I did.

THELMA Does it work?

HARRY Oh, yeh.

THELMA Aren't you clever! What a pity you haven't any lines for it.

HARRY Mebbe I will have one day. A layout, like.

THELMA You mean, when you have a home of your own?

HARRY Er, yeh, when I've got the space.

THELMA This is a nice room, though. You're comfortable here, aren't you?

HARRY It's all right.

THELMA I expect you like living here altogether. Me mam's good at looking after men.

HARRY Yeh.

THELMA I take after her for that. She's always made me learn to do things about the house.

HARRY It's useful....to know.

THELMA (*after a pause*) I saw some lovely engagement rings in town the other day. Not too expensive, but nice.

HARRY Oh, yes, well....

THELMA Funny I should be looking only the other day...I expect you get a bit lonely sometimes, on your own up here.

HARRY Oh, no. No...I like to be on me own. Think things over, like.

THELMA Well, there's no need for it, y'know. Me mam said would I ask you if you'd like to come and watch television with us. There's a big film on in a bit, and a comedy show later.

HARRY Well, thanks very much. Mebbe I will, in a bit. I've got one or two things to do just now.

THELMA (*a trifle coyly*) Well, perhaps I'd better not stop up here too long. We'll see you later, then?

HARRY Yeh, in a bit.

The door shuts. We are inside Harry's mind.

THELMA (*Echo*) They'll p'raps shine when they've had a real chance to dry.

FIRST MECH. (*Echo*) Harry's got a bit laid on at home. Haven't you Harry?

HARRY (*Echo*) I'd like to look after you all along...all along.

THELMA (*Echo*) Guess what, Mam. Me and Harry's engaged!

Pause

HARRY (*to himself*) Ruined....

Fade out.

Fade in.

The Baynes's sitting room.

Thelma and her mother are watching television.

There is a time-lag of preoccupied silence between question and answer.

MRS BAYNES What did he say?

THELMA Who?

MRS BAYNES Harry.

THELMA He said he'd be down in a bit.

MRS BAYNES Is that all?

THELMA Well, you know he never does say much.

MRS BAYNES No, there's one thing about Harry. He won't talk you to death.
Fade out.

Fade in.

The hallway.
Harry is creeping downstairs.
The living room door opens suddenly, letting out the sound of the TV set.

MRS BAYNES Oh, there you are, Harry. We've been wondering about you.
You weren't going out, were you?

HARRY Well, I just thought I. . . .

MRS BAYNES No, that's right. Come in and join the family circle. There was
no need for you to dress up in your jacket. We don't stand on
ceremony in the family and I think we can call you one of the
family now, can't we?
He follows her into the room reluctantly.
The door shuts, blocking off the sound.
Fade out.

Fade in.

The Baynes's sitting room.
Jack is following a cricket commentary on TV.
The back door opens.

THELMA *(off)* Mother! Mother, where are you? *(coming in)* Dad, where's
me mam?

JACK How do I know where she is? Let's have a bit of hush, can't we?
I can't hear what they're saying.

MRS BAYNES *(approaching)* Now then, what's all the noise about?

THELMA Mam! I've got something to show you.

MRS BAYNES Oh yes? Come in, Harry. Don't stand in the doorway like an
insurance man.

THELMA Mam. . .

MRS BAYNES Yes, I heard you. Just a minute, let's have this turned down.
She turns the TV sound down.

JACK Here! What do you think you're doing?

MRS BAYNES Making it so we can hear ourselves talk.

JACK Can't you go somewhere else to talk?

MRS BAYNES We're talking here a minute. If you can't make out what they're
doing without somebody telling you, you don't know as much

about cricket as you reckon you do.

A huge sigh from Jack Baynes.

THELMA Mam.

MRS BAYNES Yes, love. What have you got to show me?

THELMA This!

MRS BAYNES Well! I didn't know you were going out buying engagement rings.

THELMA I didn't really know if Harry meant to this afternoon.

MRS BAYNES Very nice! Here, just look at this, Jack. Show it to your dad, Thelma.

THELMA Look, Dad.

JACK (*without enthusiasm*) Very nice. It's a bit on the big side, isn't it?

HARRY That's what *I* said.

THELMA Oh, but they wanted a couple of days to alter it and I just had to show you.

MRS BAYNES Aye. . . . So now it's official.

JACK They'll never get a double bed in that room of Harry's. Nor our Thelma's either.

MRS BAYNES Who's talking about getting a double bed in?

JACK Where they going to live, then, with house prices the way they are?

THELMA (*suddenly dejected*) Oh well. We can always save up and hope for the best.

MRS BAYNES Happen you won't need to.

THELMA What do you mean?

MRS BAYNES I've been talking to Parkinson Fernside today.

JACK Parkinson Fernside?

MRS BAYNES Don't tell me you don't know who Parkinson Fernside is?

JACK Well o' course I know who he is, but I didn't know you knew him.

MRS BAYNES Me not know Parkinson Fernside? I used to go to school with him. I can remember Parkinson Fernside when he'd patches on his britches' behind. And look at him now, with half a dozen shops and property all over the place.

JACK You never told me you went to school with Parkinson Fernside.

MRS BAYNES I must have done. You couldn't have been listening. (*pause*) Why, I might have married him.

THELMA Did he ever ask you?

MRS BAYNES Well, no, not exactly. But there was a time. . . . Anyway, by the time that auntie of his died in Australia and gave him his start, I was already married to your dad.

JACK Hard lines!

MRS BAYNES Nay, it's late in the day for jealousy.

JACK *(softly)* God's truth!

MRS BAYNES He knew me, though. I was just coming out of Walshaw's when he rolled up and got out of his big motor car. He looks at me and stops, and I says, "Don't you know me, then, Parkinson?" "Of course I know you," he says. "It's Daisy Auty." That's me maiden name, you know, Harry—Auty. "It must be ten years since I saw you," he says. "More like fifteen," I told him. Anyway, he asked me how I was keeping and one thing led to another and I told him I had a daughter planning to get married.

THELMA Mam, what's all this to *do* with me and Harry getting married?

MRS BAYNES You're an impatient dolly. You won't let anybody tell a right tale.

THELMA I thought it had something to do with. . . .

MRS BAYNES What I'm trying to tell you, if you'll listen a minute, is that Parkinson's just had one of his houses come vacant and he says if you go and see his agents on Monday morning, you can have it.

HARRY To rent, you mean?

MRS BAYNES Yes, to rent.

THELMA A house! Oh, Mam, Mam, that's marvellous!

MRS BAYNES It's not a mansion, mind—just a two up and two down in Waterman Street, but it'll give you a start.

THELMA Oh, you hear that, Harry? Isn't it smashing?

HARRY Aye, aye. It sounds all right.

JACK Looks to me as if you'll be selling that motor-bike of yours to pay for furniture, Harry.

HARRY Nay. . .

THELMA Oh, we shan't sell that.

MRS BAYNES Maybe when you get on your feet you'll run to a little car.

THELMA Oh no, I like the bike. I didn't think I should, but I do now. And anyway, when the time comes, we could always fit a sidecar. *Fade out.*

Fade in.

Harry's house.

An empty room

HARRY Make sure you get your paste right up to the edges, Thelma. You missed a bit here. Just pass us your brush a minute. *(pause)* There, that's got it.

Harry descends the stepladder.

THELMA Isn't it a lovely paper, Harry? Aren't you pleased with it?

HARRY (*soberly*) Yeh, it's all right.

THELMA You know, you're so clever. I didn't know you could do decorating as well.

HARRY Aw, there's not much to it, providing you take care. The pasting's the important part. You've got to get plenty of paste right up to the edges.

THELMA I'm just getting the hang of it now we've nearly finished.

HARRY You know, you didn't ought to be wearing your engagement ring for this job.

THELMA Oh, but I like it on all the time. It reminds me.

HARRY Eh?

THELMA How lucky I am.

HARRY Oh. Still you should take care. You know it's a bit on the big side.

THELMA I think we're both lucky. I mean about getting this house. Fancy me mother just happening to hear about it like that. When I told Lottie Sharpe she turned green with envy. She's still living at home now she's married.

HARRY Lots of people have to.

THELMA Yes, I know. But we can start off in our own home, with our own furniture and everything.

HARRY Aye...it's a right load of hire purchase I've taken on.

THELMA *We've* taken on. I shall be working to help pay it off, shan't I?

HARRY Aye, I suppose so.

THELMA I think that red carpet's going to look smashing with this wallpaper. I'm glad we picked this pattern in the end.

HARRY You can never really tell till you get it on the walls.

THELMA What I think is, we ought to have the mirror over the fireplace. Or else a nice picture. They've got some lovely views in the stores in the town. Then we could have the mirror over the sideboard on that wall.

HARRY I thought you wanted the sideboard over there?

THELMA I think I've changed me mind. I'd like the settee against that window now, and the table in the middle. Then when we feel like a change we can put the settee in the middle and the table against the window. That'll be better for sitting by the fire when we're entertaining friends.

HARRY I don't know as I have any friends I want to entertain.

THELMA Well, there's always me mam and dad. And we shall get to know lots of young married couples. I might even ask Lottie and her husband round one night when we're all finished.

HARRY Aye, well let's get this last piece up.

He climbs the stepladder.

THELMA How's the time?

HARRY Nearly half-past twelve.

THELMA Ooh, hasn't the time flown. Me mam'll have the dinner waiting for us.

HARRY You get cleaned up then, while I fix this.

THELMA Righto, then.

She goes to the back door to empty the bucket.

(*off*) Can you manage?

HARRY Yeh. Nearly done.

He comes down the ladder again.

There. (*pause*) What's up, then? It's not upside down, is it?

THELMA No, it's lovely.

HARRY Aye, it's not so bad, now it's up.

THELMA Harry....

HARRY What's up?

THELMA Harry, I don't know how to tell you.

HARRY Tell me what?

THELMA Harry.... I've lost me engagement ring.

HARRY Eh?

THELMA I had it a minute since and now it's gone.

HARRY Well, have you had a look for it?

THELMA No, it's no use. I think it must have been when I was emptying the bucket. It's gone down the outside drain.

HARRY (*staggered*) Well, that's a right flaming how d'you do.

THELMA Oh, Harry, I am sorry.

HARRY It's a lot of good saying that now. I told you not ten minutes since about wearing it for mucky jobs. You were just asking to lose it. And you wouldn't let me take it to be altered either. You had to wear it as it was.

THELMA I know, Harry. I know. And I'm sorry.

HARRY What good does being bloody sorry do?

THELMA You've every right to be upset, Harry, but I'm just as sorry as you are.

HARRY As sorry as me? How can you be as sorry as me? You didn't pay for it, did you? I did. Twenty quid it cost. Nearly a week's wage, not counting overtime. Good money down the drain. (*realising the aptness*) Aye, *right* down the drain.

THELMA Can't you think of anything but the money?

HARRY What else do you expect me to think about?

THELMA You could think about me. I've said I'm sorry and you can see how upset I am, but all you can think about is the money. That's all you ever do think about—money and 'things'. You never think about people's feelings, do you? All you think about is your 'things'.

HARRY Well, what about you? What am I to you? I'm not me. I'm a husband you've caught. Summat to show off to your friends and the neighbours. Just a thing of yours.

THELMA I don't know how you can say that.

HARRY I can say it because it's true.

THELMA If that's what you think we'd better call it all off. You say I caught you—well now I'm letting you go. I don't want a husband who thinks about *things* all the time.

HARRY And what about all the furniture, and this house?

THELMA (*going*) You can give backword—or else live here by yourself. And as for your precious twenty pound—I'll pay it all back, out of me wages. Two pound a week.
She goes, slamming the door behind her.

HARRY Well, by bloody hell!
Fade out.

Fade in.

The Baynes's sitting room.
Thelma is sobbing.

MRS BAYNES It's no use making a song and dance about it now. Speak in haste, repent at leisure. You had that young man well on the way to the altar and now you've let him go.

THELMA You don't think I could marry a man who thought like that, do you?

MRS BAYNES The perfect man hasn't been born yet. All men have summat wrong with 'em. But you've got to make the best of 'em 'cos they're all we've got. And they're slippery customers an' all. They'll take all and give nowt if you let 'em. I only hope you've done nothing with Harry 'at you'll regret now.

THELMA (*renewed tears*) I wish I had, then he'd p'raps have thought about something else besides money and 'things'.
Fade out.

Fade in.

The locker room.

FOREMAN Ah, Harry. Well, I reckon it won't be long now, eh? How many more weeks of freedom?

HARRY   Eh?

FOREMAN   Before you get wed.

HARRY   I'm not getting wed now. It's all off.

FOREMAN   Is it, by gum!

HARRY   We had a row over summat.

FOREMAN   Well, I wouldn't take it too serious, Harry. Rows between engaged couples have been patched up before.

HARRY   Not this one. I never wanted to get wed, anyway. And all she wanted was a husband to show off to everybody. Any single bloke would've done.

FOREMAN   Well, I've been married twenty year, and if me and the wife had split up every time we had a few words we'd have been separated dozens of times. Still, you know your own mind best. You'll be wanting fresh digs now, I reckon?

HARRY   Aye. I've been in a commercial hotel this last couple of nights. I was wondering, Bert, if you knew anywhere cheap I could get in. I only need a place for a week or two till I get the house finished.

FOREMAN   You're keeping the house on, then?

HARRY   Aye, I'm fed up o' getting mixed up with people. If I live on me own I can do as I like.

Fade out.

Fade in.

Harry's house.

LIVERY MAN   Where do you want this standard lamp?

HARRY   Oh, anywhere'll do.

LIVERY MAN   Here in this corner suit you?

HARRY   Er, yeh. That'll be all right.

LIVERY MAN   That's the lot, then. Very nice. Now if you'll just sign for them we're all done and dusted. (*pause*) Ta. (*going*) Be seeing you then.

HARRY   So long.

LIVERY MAN   So long. Thanks very much.

He goes out through the back door.
Pause.
There is a knock on the front door. Harry opens it.

POSTMAN   Registered letter.

HARRY   Oh, thanks.

POSTMAN   Sign here, please. Just moved in, have you?

HARRY   Yeh, just today.

POSTMAN   Very nice. Be seeing you, then. So long.

HARRY Cheerio.

The door closes. Harry tears the envelope open.

(*to himself*) Two quid.

THELMA (*Echo*) As for your precious twenty pound—I'll pay it all back, out of me wages. Two pound a week.

Fade out.

Fade in.

The locker room.

FIRST MECH. What about a lift into town, Harry?

HARRY If you like. I can't take you both, though.

FIRST MECH. Aw, I reckon I might as well go down on the bus with Jeff.

SECOND MECH. You'll be going home to a cold house, Harry.

FIRST MECH. Oh, he's used to that by now.

SECOND MECH. You'll have your own tea to get an' all.

HARRY Don't you worry. I can manage.

FIRST MECH. Aye, we know you're very efficient. We were wondering when you were going to have your party. Leaving it a bit late, aren't you?

HARRY What party?

FIRST MECH. Your house-warming.

HARRY I can see that coming off.

SECOND MECH. You say the word, Harry, and we'll get a few of the lads together with a crate o' beer, and come down to cheer you up.

HARRY You think I'm daft enough to get you lot down there.

SECOND MECH. Aw, now we know how to behave in people's houses, Harry. Tell you what, we could line up a few women as well.

FIRST MECH. Don't talk to Harry about women. He's off 'em.

SECOND MECH. Why's he off 'em?

FIRST MECH. He had a ghastly experience not long since. A narrow escape. There's no flies on Harry, though. He got out of it. Didn't you, Harry?

HARRY What're you talking about now?

FIRST MECH. Thelma. Thelma Baynes. Everybody knows her and her mother nearly hooked you. I saw her the other night, dancing at the Gala Rooms. New hair style, platform-soled shoes. Didn't recognise her at first. She's come out of her shell good an' proper. (*suggestively*) Reckon somebody must have wakened her up and shown her the joys of life.

HARRY Look, why don't you try shutting up?

FIRST MECH. What have I said now?

HARRY You've said too much. You're allus talking, you and your mate here. You're like a pair of bloody little dogs yapping about the place. One of these days somebody'll give you a good straight kick where it hurts.

FIRST MECH. Now there's no need to get nasty.

HARRY I feel nasty. So you'd better start minding your own business, or I'll be after you. One at a time or both at once, it won't bother me. But I'll sort the pair of you out if you don't stop it off.
He kicks the motor-bike engine off.

FIRST MECH. If that's the way you want it to be, Harry.

HARRY That's the way I want it to be, so just think on.
The motor-bike moves off.

FIRST MECH. That's the way he wants it to be, Jeff. So just think on.
Fade out.

Fade in.

Harry's house.
He opens the door.

MRS KITSON Oh, there you are.

HARRY Hello, Mrs Kitson. What are you doing here at this time o' day?

MRS KITSON I wanted to have a word with you. I didn't know you'd be so late.

HARRY I've been doing a bit of overtime. And you've laid the table. You shouldn't have started doing all that.

MRS KITSON Oh, it's no bother. I like to keep me hands occupied. What will you be fancying for your tea?

HARRY Oh, I've a bit o' stew left to warm up. But don't you bother. I don't pay you to cook for me. What was it you wanted to see me about?

MRS KITSON Well, I don't like to say it, but I haven't been too well lately. It's me back, y'know. It looks as if I shall have to reduce me commitments.

HARRY You mean you'll have to stop cleaning for me?

MRS KITSON That's about the size of it. And you being my last client, and only two mornings a week with laundry. . . .

HARRY Oh aye, aye. You can't let your old customers down.

MRS KITSON Such a shame, really, because I've always liked coming here. You've got a lovely home and it's all so new it takes hardly any seeing to at all. I was saying to a cousin of mine only the other week 'at it was just like a furniture shop window. You'd think nobody lived here at all. 'Course, you take care of your things and it's not as if you'd a couple of bairns crawling about and putting their sticky fingers on everything. I always say 'at married couples have to buy two homes in a lifetime—one when they get wed and another when the bairns grow up and leave.

HARRY Er, I wonder, do you think you could find somebody else to do it?

MRS KITSON Well, I'll try me best. I'll try not to leave you in the lurch.

HARRY Oh, it's not a matter of that. I mean, I could manage all right meself. You say yourself it takes no looking after.

MRS KITSON Aye, but a man doesn't want to start cleaning and washing when he's done his day's work. No, I'll hang on for a while and see what I can fix up. It's a shame you have to live in such a nice place on your own. The lass 'at let you down ought to have her head examined.

HARRY Well, it wasn't exactly. . . .

MRS KITSON Oh, I know her. I know her *and* her mother. Have for years. You don't have to say anything. Them that knows knows. Anyway, I shall have to be off. I'll do me best to get you fixed up. Ta-ra.

HARRY Well, thanks anyway.

MRS KITSON (*going*) Oh, and there's a registered letter on the sideboard. The postman brought it and I signed for it.

HARRY Thanks. I know what it'll be.

She goes out.

MRS KITSON Ta-ra then.

HARRY Ta-ra.

The door shuts. He rips the envelope open.

THELMA (*Echo*) Two pound a week, Harry. Two pound a week.

SECOND MECH. (*Echo*) You'll be going home to a cold house, Harry.

HARRY (*Echo*) If I live on me own I can do as I like.

Fade out.

Fade in.

The garage.

Machinery in the background.

HARRY Ouch! That stings.

FOREMAN It will do. It's deep. You need a couple of stitches in it.

FIRST MECH. Want me to run you round to hospital on your bike, Harry?

FOREMAN I'll run him round in the car when I've bandaged his hand. You'd be better off out there getting some work done.

FIRST MECH. (*going*) Just trying to help, that's all. Let's hope they don't have to amputate.

HARRY I don't know how it happened.

FOREMAN You couldn't have been watching what you were doing, lad.

HARRY I suppose I must have had summat else on me mind.

FOREMAN It's all this living on your own. It makes you broody.

HARRY I allus thought I'd like living on me own.

FOREMAN Every man to his taste. But it'd drive me up the wall, having to do everything for meself.

HARRY Ah, well, I have a woman who cleans and washes for me.

FOREMAN Aye, well, that's not what you'd call company, is it? How does that feel? It's not too tight?

HARRY No, it's not so bad.

Fade out.

Fade in.

Harry's house.

He opens the front door.

HARRY Hello! Anybody there? (*pause*) Mrs Kitson?

The inner door opens.

THELMA Hello, Harry.

HARRY Thelma! What are you doing here? Where's Mrs Kitson?

THELMA She's not coming now. She hasn't been coming for a fortnight.

HARRY But you're not my cleaning...?

THELMA Yes, I am. I've got this for you. I was going to post it but I may as well give it to you now. That makes twenty.

HARRY Aye, right, er, thanks.

THELMA Ooh, whatever have you done to your hand?

HARRY Oh, I had a bit of an accident at work.

THELMA Does it hurt?

HARRY It's all right.

THELMA You should be holding it up, not in your pocket, with all the blood running to it.

HARRY Don't fuss yourself. It's not major surgery.

THELMA (*fondly*) You are a funny lad, Harry.

HARRY Never mind funny lad. You haven't told me what you're doing here yet.

THELMA Well, me mam and me were talking to Mrs Kitson on the market and she mentioned she was looking for somebody. So I said I'd come meself if she kept quiet about it.

HARRY But what about your job?

THELMA We had some short time and they laid a few of us off. They said they might be able to take us back in a bit.

HARRY What I don't understand is why you wanted to come and do for me.

THELMA Oh, I don't know. I suppose I wanted to see the place after it was finished...see how you were getting on. I've been thinking about you.

HARRY Is this my clean washing?

THELMA Yes, I ironed it this morning. You need some new underwear.

HARRY I know. I was going to get round to it this weekend.

THELMA Well, I've finished for today, so I may as well get off.... If you don't like the idea of me coming in you've only to say so.

HARRY No...no. As a matter of fact, I've been thinking about *you*.

THELMA Have you, Harry?

HARRY I was thinking about you this morning when I gashed me hand.

THELMA Ooh, I am sorry, Harry.

HARRY Oh, I'm not blaming you for it. It was me own fault. Anyway, what do you think to it here downstairs, now it's finished?

THELMA It's lovely.

HARRY Just how you imagined, is it?

THELMA Oh, a lot better.

HARRY Aye, I suppose it does look nice. Mrs Kitson was saying it looked like a furniture-shop window. Just as if nobody lived here at all. A man on his own can't make a place home. I reckon it wants somebody to look after it all the time—a woman's touch.

THELMA Yes, every house needs that.

HARRY As a matter of fact, I've thought many a time, just lately, that I'm sorry we fell out like we did.

THELMA Have you really, Harry?

HARRY And I was wondering. About this place, y'know, I was thinking, like....

THELMA What were you thinking, Harry?

HARRY Well, wondering like, if you'd still like to...well you know....

THELMA I won't be somebody just to look after your things, Harry.

HARRY No, I don't mean that....Oh, hell...what I mean is, I thought I'd like living on me own and I would have done at one time, but I don't like it now and the reason for that is because I've been thinking about you.

THELMA You're sure you're not just saying all that because you've found me here and you want to be nice to me.

HARRY No, honest. Look, I'll show you....There. See?

THELMA Ooh! What a lovely ring! How long have you had that?

HARRY I've been carrying it about with me for a fortnight, trying to pluck up the courage to come and ask you to have it.

THELMA Ooh, Harry! (*slyly*) It didn't take you long to spend my twenty pounds.

HARRY Twenty quid be blowed. Thirty-two.

THELMA Oh. Well, if it's worth all that, you'd better put it where it won't get lost. (*laughs*) Oh, it's a bit tight!

HARRY I thought we'd better be on the safe side this time.

THELMA Oh, Harry, I do love you.

HARRY Do you? Well, come on then, give us a kiss.

Fade out.

There's No Point In Arguing The Toss

Don Haworth

The Cast

George

Fairground Attendant

Fred

Turnstile Woman

Woman in the Fairground

Man in the Fairground

An Irishman

The Gateman

First Bus Conductor

Smith

Jones

Harris

Crocker

Second Bus Conductor

An Inspector

Fred's Mum

There's No Point
In Arguing The Toss
Don Haworth

If you hear somebody saying "it's what he would have wanted" you can be fairly sure that the person referred to is dead and that the speaker is trying to drum up support for some action which doesn't meet with general approval.

When Dad drops dead during a ride on the ghost train on one of the regular Saturday outings which he shares with his sons Fred and George, they spend only a moment wondering if they should call an ambulance or a taxi before deciding that Dad, or at least his mortal remains, should make his last journey home in the usual way—the way he would have wanted—on the bus.

This gets them mixed up with a crowd of boisterous football supporters. During the journey one of them takes it upon himself to instil a bit of respect into the crowd and leads them in a short version of a hymn well known to football supporters, Abide With Me. The occasion prompts Fred to remember with some nostalgia incidents from his childhood and casts a light on his relationship with his father.

Although the happenings of that Saturday may appear funny or bizarre to the casual onlooker, George tells the story with a straight face: "I'm not saying it's victory over death or any of that crap but it does make folk less of a complete gonner if you take the trouble to persist in what they'd have been doing if they hadn't snuffed it."

(*Laughter of the mechanical laughing clown. Other fairground sounds. The laughing clown again. Shrieks, groans, laughter of the ghost train. The sound of its cars. More remotely, other fairground sounds*)

GEORGE Of course after the event everybody's very wise and fruity about what you should have done and what you shouldn't have done. We shouldn't have let our dad go on the ghost train. We take the point. But he wasn't what you'd call a nervous type and I've never heard before of anybody being frightened to death. I mean literally frightened to death. He must have been dead the first time round, but me and our Fred were some distance away chatting up some birds and we just thought he was staying on for another ride. It's funny the attendant didn't spot it, because at that rate you could have people paying a shilling and riding round and round all day. Anyway the next time round we were up by the rails and the attendant was a bit more on his toes.

ATTENDANT Tnere's a gentleman here's passed on—

GEORGE —the attendant said.

FRED He's our dad—

GEORGE —our Fred said.

ATTENDANT I extend my personal sympathy but the company holds itself in no way responsible for loss, damage, injury or accident however incurred.

FRED All right, all right.

ATTENDANT It's displayed there and printed on the back of the ticket.

FRED He can't read, he's dead. And we don't want to argue the toss.

ATTENDANT There's no toss to be argued. I extend my personal sympathy without prejudice to the fact that the company holds itself in no way responsible.

FRED All right. Let's get round to him.

ATTENDANT You can't come through the turnstile without paying. It registers and it's checked against the cash.

FRED How much?

ŔNSTILE WOMAN Is there two of you? Two shillings.
(*money put down. Turnstile clicks*)

ATTENDANT There's nothing in the form of a platform ticket here so if you pass through the turnstile at all you've got to pay the full price for a ride.

FRED We'll forgo the privilege. We just want to get him home.

ATTENDANT He'll have to go in the accident book.

FRED It's not an accident, man; he's dead.

ATTENDANT We don't keep a death book. Accidents include death but deaths don't include accidents.

FRED It's not necessarily so either way.

ATTENDANT There are people waiting for a ride. It's neither the time nor the place for a barrack-room lawyer.

FRED We're not barrack-room lawyers. We're the next of kin of the deceased.

ATTENDANT Are you saying that those propositions are mutually exclusive?

FRED We're not saying anything. We don't want to argue the toss.

GEORGE But that's exactly what they were doing—our Fred and the attendant—arguing the toss, and the car set off again before

anybody could press the button or whatever stops it, and our dad went sailing round for another lap.
(*ghost train running, loud speaker, whoops, shrieks, laughter*)
It's pretty macabre stuff having a real live corpse riding round on the ghost train—or rather a real dead corpse—and I suppose comical if you're that way inclined, but me and our Fred felt ridiculous standing there on the platform and by the time he came round again a fair old crowd had collected at the rail.

FRED Disperse—

GEORGE —our Fred said, but they didn't seem to understand the word. He rephrased it with two short words they did understand, and immediately there was a hullabaloo.
(*protesting voices*)

WOMAN He worked for you when you were little, didn't he, and you using language in front of his mortal remains.

MAN With ladies present.

WOMAN To say nothing of ladies being present. It's a very unsavoury incident.

GEORGE They went on chewing the rag and the attendant insisted on putting our dad's particulars down in his book, then some Paddy at the back of the crowd felt the time ripe to make himself heard.

IRISHMAN He's in need of a priest.

WOMAN Or a clergyman of some kind or another.

MAN Denomination.

WOMAN A man of God of one description or another.

MAN Denomination. That's the correct word in this context.

FRED Thanks, but he never went in for that kind of thing.

WOMAN That's his loss. This is exactly the kind of situation where you need the consolation of religious faith.

FRED Thanks. We don't want to argue the toss.

MAN You've got to believe in the hereafter and reunion with loved ones. You can't just think he's had his chips, that's his lot. Life would become meaningless.

IRISHMAN Shouldn't the police be summoned?

MAN You can summon them but they won't come. They're all en route for the football match. There are none left to deal with untoward incidents in other parts of the city.

FRED It's not an untoward incident. He's passed on. It comes to us all, George, take his weight on your shoulder.

GEORGE And our Fred lifted him gently and with such care that they suddenly went quiet and I couldn't see them anyway for tears

35

and I can't remember anything till we got to the gate, though we must have walked half a mile humping him through the side-shows, being stared at in passing by people who probably thought nothing more about it. The gateman was a fat little bloke with war medal ribbons and he launched out in a reasonably sympathetic manner.

GATEMAN Hard luck. How did he cop it?

FRED On the ghost train.

GATEMAN You never know which one has your number on it, as it says in the Good Book. Hard luck.

GEORGE And he fished out his key to open the big double gates they let charabanc parties in through.

FRED No ostentation, please. We'll go through the little gate for pedestrians.

GATEMAN He's not a pedestrian.

FRED He's not a coach party either.

GATEMAN You'll wear his boot toes out humping him along like that.

FRED Are they your boots?

GATEMAN I'm not saying—

FRED Well, belt up then.

GEORGE And it was on this acrimonious note that we left the amusement park and went to wait for the bus. You might think that in the circumstances we'd have gone in for a bit of private transport, a taxi or perhaps given a van driver a quid to whip him home. But the point is we'd always come out together on the bus with Red Rover tickets and we'd always gone home together on the bus. It was a habit that we'd all joined in and it would have been letting him down to have abruptly discontinued the programme just because he'd passed on. You hear old birds at a funeral when they get maudlin say "He'd have liked that". What the thing is is neither here nor there. They mean that they're carrying on at something regardless, same as if the deceased wasn't deceased. I'm not saying it's victory over death, but it does make folk less of a complete goner if you take the trouble to persist in what they'd have been doing if they hadn't snuffed it. If that's too involved for you, never mind. I'm just explaining why we went on the bus. Now what follows is about bus conductors and I know it is bound to stir up the dirt with the Transport and General Workers' Union. The fact remains that a certain percentage of bus conductors are rotten. You see a woman, say, with two kiddies and a fold-up pram struggling to get into the bus and they not only leave her to it but make her all flushed and embarrassed by standing there looking impatient with their thumb on the bell. I'm not saying all conductors, but the fact is they just don't get officer material on the buses. The hours and wages are simply not conducive.

(bus approaching)

First it was the 72X.

(bus stops)

CONDUCTOR   No drunks.

FRED   He's not drunk, he's dead.

CONDUCTOR   The same rule applies.

FRED   What rule?

CONDUCTOR   The management reserve the right of admission.

FRED   That doesn't apply to the buses.

CONDUCTOR   It does apply to the buses.

FRED   Where is it stated?

CONDUCTOR   I'm stating it.

FRED   He has the right to travel on the bus.

CONDUCTOR   The only people that have the right to travel on any bus is the people that hold tickets for the journey in question.

FRED   Right, that's us. We all have Red Rovers.

CONDUCTOR   Use them on the next bus. We've already been overtaken by the 72 that's three behind us. Get a taxi.

(bell rings, bus goes)

GEORGE   Anything in fact but take a bit of responsibility himself. That's what I meant about not getting officer material on the buses. Missing this 72X put us in a predicament because the best bet then was the 104, which went into the city centre where the football specials waited and there was already a long queue for it, football supporters with scarves and rattles and toppers and whatnot.

(queue sings ee-aye-addy-ho we're going to win the cup. Rattles sound)

It had come on raining a bit and we weren't going to hump our dad to the end of the queue. At the same time it wasn't right for us to muscle in at the top, and given a situation of this kind and people in a Saturday afternoon mood you can't calmly negotiate at what point of the queue you ought to enter it as a special privilege in the circumstances. So we stood at the top of the queue and there was a certain amount of chunnering, which is understandable. People at the bottom of the queue craned forward to see what was going on and an argument broke out some distance down the line when we took the weight off our shoulders a bit by propping our dad against the bus stop.

SMITH Was he en route for the match?

FRED No, he'd been on the ghost train.

SMITH He didn't miss his bit of pleasure then.

FRED No.

SMITH You know, it occurred after rather than before. At a big match, say, a lot get carried out even before the teams appear, so they have all the trouble of getting dolled up and changing buses and perhaps buying a programme and then not being spared to witness the event alluded to in the programme. Sometimes they've a hell of a job to get the programme out of their grasp.

FRED It could have happened a lot worse.

SMITH He'd had his ride.

FRED Three for the price of one.

SMITH Fair enough. And he'd had his Saturday dinner.

FRED No. Our mum works Saturday mornings. We just have a bit of breaky, then we come out with a Red Rover and tour up and down, then my mum has a decent blow-out ready for us when we get back.

SMITH And that's been a ritual like?

FRED Every Saturday since our George could walk. Well, I'm saying every Saturday but only within reason. Not if it's pissing down.

SMITH There's no point in getting soaked.

FRED Or if we have folk coming to the house.

SMITH You've stuck together as a family.

FRED Correct. Some blokes are same as lodgers. In for meals then cheerio till bedtime. Some blokes you see them trailing round shopping with birds with rollers in their hair, looking at furniture and all that. Anything but go out with their own family.

SMITH Have a snout.

FRED Don't smoke, thanks.

SMITH Did he smoke?

FRED No.

SMITH See, you can renounce all worldly pleasures, then it comes like that.

FRED Being a non-smoker doesn't necessarily make him into a saint.

SMITH No, but the point remains. . . . You could call an ambulance.

FRED No, thanks.

SMITH It costs nothing. Just threepence for the call.

FRED We'll go on the bus.

SMITH Or you could dial 999 and have it entirely buckshee.

FRED That's not the point. The point is that we've come out together every Saturday.

SMITH (*sympathetically*) Bar when it was pissing down or you had folks coming.

FRED And we've been round together on the Red Rover to lots of places—places that lots of folks in this city don't know about even though they're living on top of them—and we've gone home together. Way things has turned out this is the last jaunt and we owe it to him to take him home in a normal decent manner on the bus.

SMITH Fair enough. I admire you for it. If more young fellows had your sentiments we wouldn't have all these unofficial strikes to contend with...or the balance of payments...or all these immigrants coming in, reducing the value of property. I'll put a word in for you.

FRED We're against radical discrimination.

SMITH All the same. (*shouts*) Listen...Listen...Hold that rattle still, son...Listen. There's a gentleman here had an accident so let's not have the usual stampede please when the bus draws up.

JONES (*distant*) What's up with him?

SMITH (*shouts*) He's had an accident.

JONES Has he passed out?

SMITH (*shouting*) On or over rather than out.

HARRIS Should get an ambulance.

JONES Call a taxi.

SMITH (*shouts*) And his son here wishes to take him home on the bus in the normal manner. So no stampeding, please. (*speaks*) You'll be all right. I was a respected member of the Ladybrook Brass Band for seventeen years.

(*bus approaching*)

(*shouts*) All right, it's coming. It's not an electric hare so don't bound out of the trap.

(*bus stops. Queue surges*)

Hold it, hold it.

CONDUCTOR Upstairs, all of you.

SMITH Right, conductor. There's a gentleman here passed on.

CONDUCTOR Hump him upstairs.

FRED He's a non-smoker.

CONDUCTOR Look, it's a concession to let him on at all in that state. The upper saloon, please. We've already...

FRED I know.

CONDUCTOR You know what?

FRED You've already been overtaken by the bus that's two behind.

CONDUCTOR A bit fly, eh? This isn't a hearse, you know. You can take your pick—upstairs or wait for the next bus.

HARRIS Come on. Get on with it.

SMITH Hold it, hold it. Give him air.

HARRIS What's he want air for?

SMITH He wants respect.

HARRIS You said air.

SMITH Look, I was in the Ladybrook Brass Band for seventeen years.

GEORGE Well, the repartee continued at roughly this level with a certain amount of jostling and pushing and the conductor standing there impatient with his thumb on the bell, as I mentioned before, until our Fred took hold of our dad under the arms and started to struggle backwards upstairs with him.
(*feet on the steps*)

FRED Guide his feet, George.

GEORGE And there was something about the way he lifted our dad that made them all go quiet—same as with the crowd when he humped him out of the ghost train. It was the expression on his face like you see on madonnas in art galleries. Quiet—reposeful rather. Dedicated. Those are the words. As if there was nobody within a mile of us. I could see them all pushing and gawping and having their bits of arguments in the mirror when we went round the bend on the stairs. Our Fred couldn't see the mirror because he was backing up, but even if he could he wouldn't have looked into it because all his heart was in getting our dad upstairs and you would have thought he was deaf for all the notice he took of the stir we created on the upper deck.

CROCKER Is that a corpse you've got there?

GEORGE He simply didn't hear. Some uncouth merchant damn nearly legged him up with a dog lead, shifting hastily with his dog, like they were all doing—dogs or no dogs—to the seats at the front. Our Fred simply didn't notice. He plonked our dad down by the window and sat beside him and nodded me into the seat in front.
(*bell rings. Bus moves off*)
The man who had been in the brass band parked himself beside me.

SMITH They're a good lot, United supporters. You can always rely on them to act in a restraintful manner in a case of this sort. They'd sing a hymn if I asked them.

FRED Thanks, but we'll take it as read.

SMITH No, seriously. They all know 'Abide with Me'. (*shouts*) You all know 'Abide with Me'. (*speaks*) They sing it at the Cup Final.

GEORGE And he took a lad's rattle and began to conduct.

SMITH (*sings*) 'Abide with Me, fast falls the eventide,
(*other voices join in increasingly*)
The darkness deepens, Lord with me abide.
When other helpers fail and comforts flee
Help of the helpless, O abide with me.'
(*alone*) 'I need thy presence every passing hour
(*Smith continues uncertainly beneath narration*)

GEORGE But the rest of them didn't know the words of the second verse
and the man from the brass band was left warbling on his tod till
our Fred brought the axe down on proceedings.

FRED All right. That'll do. You've made your point. Thank you.

GEORGE The man from the brass band memowed them to fill up the seats
round us. They had left a kind of *cordon sanitaire* round us which
could have made us feel conspicuous but, fair play, they did
move in upon request and this confirmed the man from the band
in the role he'd taken upon himself as our handler or impresario
or PRO or something.

SMITH These lads have been telling me they've been out with their dad
every Saturday, come hell or high water, bar when it's literally
pissing down or they have folks coming. I'll bet if you added it
all up he's clocked up a fair old mileage riding round on the
ghost train.

FRED We haven't come here all that often.

SMITH See, living opposite the amusement park I don't think I've been
inside it since I took my sister's kiddie on and he's an insurance
agent now.

HARRIS (*to boys*) Where did you go then?

SMITH I'm making the point that, living on the doorstep, you get blasé,
though they come in charabanc loads from miles away, Yorkshire, all sorts of queer places.

HARRIS Where did you go then besides the fun fair?
(*pause*)

JONES The lad doesn't want to talk.

FRED It's not that. Put baldly like that it's hard to remember. Museums
and places.

HARRIS Art galleries?

FRED Like in one museum there's a tree made out of stone, fossil—
dating back to the Ice Age.

HARRIS There were no trees in the Ice Age.

FRED There was this tree because it's in the museum.

HARRIS Not in the Ice Age.

FRED If you want an argument you'd better go and argue with the

41

curator.

HARRIS There was nothing grew in the Ice Age. It was all just ice as the name infers, entirely barren.

JONES The lad doesn't want to haggle about fossils at a time like this.

FRED It's not that, I just haven't got the background. The little picture—plaque is it?—at the bottom said it grew in the Ice Age. I'm only telling you what the plaque said. I wasn't there myself.

SMITH It'll be a shock to your mum. Was he in the war?

FRED He was on munitions. He never did anything. He drifted in and out of jobs and on the public assistance, but he was the life and soul of everything. Everybody knew him for miles round. He was pleased with everything just like a little kid. Same as with this tree. He had no background either but he'd have put it better than me.

HARRIS It couldn't have grown in the Ice Age.

FRED Well, you say that to me and I think, 'all right, get stuffed'. But my dad had a way with him. He'd agree with folk whatever they said but they'd finish up agreeing with him. That doesn't make sense, does it?

GEORGE I don't think our Fred had ever spoken two consecutive sentences about our dad before. It was amazing seeing him sitting there by our dad holding forth glibly on all manner of topics.

JONES I understand. He was a charming man. A gentleman.

FRED Outside the house.

JONES He was a good dad to you.

FRED He was rotten at home.

SMITH You're upset, lad.

CONDUCTOR Any more fares please.

GEORGE Our Fred held the three Red Rovers up without thinking about it and he went on talking regardless of the audience, the same as he'd humped our dad up the stairs, heedless of people peering and boggling, and they were shuffling about in their seats and you could see they felt the time ripe to drop the subject but once he'd got under way it just didn't occur to our Fred that it was unsuitable to ventilate his thoughts on private matters to a load of football supporters sitting on top of a bus with our dad cooling off.

SMITH Treat every man according to his deserts and we'd all get a right hammering, as Shakespeare said.

FRED That's not the point.

SMITH The point is you're inferring he was strict with you. He probably conceived it his duty. But on your own admission he's been romping round town with you every Saturday, bar certain honourable exceptions, seeing a bit of life.

FRED And a bit of death now.

SMITH Today's an exception. It's none of my business but I don't see what you're holding against him.

FRED All right. I don't want to argue the toss.

SMITH You'll feel better when you get home.

FRED It won't alter the record.

SMITH You'll feel different about it when you get older.

FRED What I feel isn't the point. It's just a sad dismal record for him to have to live with.

GEORGE Well, there was a pause. You could see the point registering even on the thickest of the persons present that our dad didn't have to live with his record. That is just what he didn't have to do, having passed on. You could see the brass band man wanted to do whatever was kindest, to let the subject drop or give our Fred a sympathetic hearing, whichever was for the best. He made a couple of false starts then said:

SMITH Is it a police record like you're alluding to?

FRED No, he had no police record. I mean the neighbours called the police dozens of times but we weren't taken down to the station for a hammering or hauled in front of a judge or anything like that. Domestics—the police just don't want to know. All right, they'd say, we don't want to know but cut out scrapping round the happy home. It upsets the old ladies next door.

SMITH Who was scrapping then?

FRED Me and my dad. Our George here had a few bouts with him but usually me and my dad.

SMITH And it rattled the old ladies next door?

FRED Next door but one actually. Next door the poor beggar's deaf so it didn't worry him.

SMITH He was impervious to bumping and banging.

FRED That's it, bumping and banging. He'd throw anything. He's smashed everything in the house that could be thrown.

SMITH He was handy with the furniture then?

FRED Stools and chairs mainly. He'd ram you up against the wall with the table, then hurl anything he could lay his hands to. He'd have you fixed like a clay pipe in a shooting gallery and he'd cob everything.

SMITH Was he always like that?

FRED No, when I was little he just used his fists but once I started fighting back—when I was fifteen or so I realised he was careless with his right elbow. He carried it high, you know, not tucked in, so I thought right I'll stop him with one in the guts. It knocked the wind out of him. You'd have thought a balloon had been let down. He was still unsteady on his pins next morning.

SMITH And you rue it now, belting your dad?

FRED Yes, I rued it and he rued it, but it didn't stop us from sailing in next time. See, our George here with being the youngest hasn't had nearly the same amount of fighting in the home. I think he thought we enjoyed it, you know did it for fun. My mum's brothers would come round and the police, and they'd all say, be reasonable, cut out the scrapping round the happy home. But he couldn't help it because he'd always thumped me and once I'd put him down for the count I understood exactly how he felt. You think, how awful and after all he's done for me, and you get so screwed up that you've just got to belt him again.

SMITH Did you never really get on with him?

FRED I wouldn't be sitting here with him now if I didn't get on with him.

JONES Human relationships are never simple.

SMITH Fair point. It's just that it's not usual to elaborate to a bus load of strangers.

FRED Well, isn't it? I mean how often have you travelled on a bus with a corpse and his relatives?

SMITH No, it just seems a bit clinical trotting out his weak points and him just passed on.

FRED Passing on doesn't make him a saint. A lot of people pass on but only a few of them get registered as saints.

JONES I'm on your side. You want to take him home in a normal way on the bus and you don't want him lost in encomium or eulogy.

FRED What's that?

JONES The old guguffle. We shall not see his like again and all that rubbish. I remember when we put my uncle up the chimney they got in a proper qualified reverend, C of E, and he launched into a eulogistic description of my uncle that damn near annihilated the poor old bastard's memory. He used to dope dogs.

SMITH You're not saying this gentleman here was a dog doper?

JONES Who said I was saying he was a dog doper?

SMITH You made an allusion.

JONES To my own uncle.

SMITH Your dad didn't dope dogs, did he?

FRED No.

SMITH (*to Jones*) Are you convinced?

JONES I take his word. The point is—

SMITH Fair enough then. Dog doping doesn't enter into this gentleman's record in any shape or form. You're out of order.

JONES I'm not out of order. You were saying why bring up all the dirt and I'm giving you my answer. This lad obviously loves his dad and he doesn't want the memory of him lost under a load of hypocrisy. His dad's all right to him exactly as he was, faults and all.

SMITH But he wasn't a dog doper. Agreed he was a bit rough about the house but there's no question of doping dogs. It's not germane.

JONES All right. All right. He did well for you in many directions, didn't he?

FRED I can't think of any offhand, but that's damn all to do with whether you love somebody or not. He mucked everything up.

JONES Not everything surely. He knocked the premises about a bit, but you've grown up strong and reasonably educated.

FRED I'm not reasonably educated. As I said I've got no background. If some bloke says trees didn't grow in the Ice Age—

HARRIS They didn't. Entirely barren—

FRED I haven't got the background to argue the toss.

JONES Whose fault is that?

FRED Same as with busting up the happy home, mine and his between us. Funny thing we had a 'home, sweet home' thing done in fretwork, craftsmanship and all that, that hung on the wall. He splintered it over my head.

SMITH A bit symbolical like?

FRED That's the point. The 'sweet' was cracked right across, being in the middle, so for a lark our George here cut it out and stuck the ends together so it said 'home home' and you can see the mark on the wall from where it used to be longer. My mum christened it 'home, home on the range'.

SMITH I know, I know. (*sings*) 'Home, home on the range.'
(*others join in increasingly*)
'Where the deer and the antelope play
Where seldom is heard
A discouraging word
And the skies are not cloudy all day.'
(*general applause. Sound of rattles. Conductor pounds upstairs*)

CONDUCTOR Cut it out. No more singing.

SMITH You can't enforce that, conductor.

CONDUCTOR Behaving in a riotous manner. There's ladies downstairs.

VOICE Send 'em up then.

(*general assent and laughter*)

CONDUCTOR I've let you bring your corpse on, but don't push it or we'll end up driving round to Lloyd George Road police station.

(*cries of dissent and abuse*)

I've told you. We did it a couple of weeks ago. We'll do it again. Grown men!

(*more dissent and abuse. Conductor clumps downstairs*)

JONES I wasn't here. What happened?

HARRIS We was late for the match.

SMITH They pulled up outside Lloyd George Road police station and the bobbies came out in their braces and sorted a few hooligans out.

CROCKER What do you mean hooligans? My brother was amongst those remanded in custody.

SMITH They were all young lads.

CROCKER That doesn't make 'em hooligans. He's earning £18 a week on a lathe.

HARRIS It doesn't follow. My brother worked a lathe but he finished up marrying a woman out of a circus.

CROCKER What's that got to do with it?

HARRIS He worked a lathe but his artistic inclinations put him on wrong lines notwithstanding.

CROCKER My brother has no artistic inclinations.

HARRIS Well my brother had. He'd sit down for hours on end and play novenas on his shillelagh.

CROCKER Aaaar, he's half way round.

HARRIS I'll be down there in a minute.

(*conductor clumping upstairs*)

CONDUCTOR Did you not hear what I said about driving round to Lloyd George Road police station?

(*silence*)

All right then, watch it. This bringing a corpse on public transport is going to be reported anyway.

(*silence. He clumps down*)

JONES (*to be kind and occupy Fred's attention*) What was that then you was saying about your education being neglected?

FRED I didn't pass my eleven plus that's all.

JONES You think a more stable home, so to speak, would have made the difference?

FRED It wasn't that. In his own way he was trying to help me. Like he was very glib and top of the morning and all the rest of it outside the home, but inside we never had what you might call close conversations. You know, I used to think when we were out and he had everybody laughing and really interested himself in all sorts of things, you know I used to think if only I could have him like that to myself. But once we got over the threshold he said virtually damn all. Like a comedian. You meet him in private life off the stage and he's just like anybody else. He has to have an audience to come alive.

JONES And that affected your education.

FRED No, well like an exception to saying damn all, he gave me a bit of an address, a long speech really, my mother had put him up to it, when I was doing my eleven plus. He kept drying up and he didn't know where to look and I didn't know where to look but he stuck at it and ploughed on ad infinitum.

JONES It's understandable. He might have been a bit garrulous—

FRED What's that?

JONES Went rabbiting on.

FRED That's what I'm saying.

JONES But he was trying to give you the benefit of his experience.

FRED I'm not denying that. The point is what he was on about. He intended it just to be encouraging but he went on about how he was a failure and he didn't have no opportunities and what did I think he felt when other fathers could take their children away on holidays, humping their luggage to the bus stop and some of them bowling away in secondhand cars, you know one owner, careful old lady then you find it's been used in a bank robbery.

SMITH I'm getting a bit lost.

JONES The thread was that his brief address put you off your stroke.

FRED It wasn't brief, but he said: "Look, Fred, don't be a layabout like me. Pass this here examination and make a man of yourself." I was eleven years old at the time.

JONES What's wrong with that?

FRED As you said yourself it put me off my stroke. I hadn't done no homework. The telly's on all the time and you can't get on the table when he's in. He's always brewing up and cooking himself an egg or something.

JONES (*kindly*) You won't have that trouble any more ... I shouldn't have said that; it was tactless.

FRED It's quite true. But that wasn't the point. See, if I'd have passed he'd have gone round crowing to people. "Our Fred's passed for the grammar school" and, say on Saturdays, he'd have had me dolled up in grammar school gear telling the museum curator and the ghost train bloke and whatnot "Our Fred's at the grammar school studying Latin and pyrotechnics and God knows what".

JONES He'd have a right to be proud of you.

FRED That's what I thought. He thumps me round the happy home or he sits there brewing up and saying damn all, then he wants me to perform at the eleven plus to give his own ego a bit of a face lift.

JONES There's another side to it.

FRED I'm coming to it. It's not like consistent with what I said. In fact it's the opposite but nevertheless it applies. I pitched up for the exam at the stated time and a little bloke with a ginger moustache starts laying down the law. "Don't turn the question paper over till I fire the gun. Don't speak to your neighbour. Don't write in the left-hand margin. Don't do this, don't do that, don't breathe.

So I thought, to hell with 'em. There was something queer about the classroom. I don't mean the desks being in single file and the floor being swept clean for once and this little bloke with the ginger moustache not being our regular teacher. So I let him rant on—I'd no option anyway—and I tried to figure out what it was, you know queer. Well, it was right in front of me. I could see it all the time, but it startled me. All the blackboards were absolutely blank. There wasn't a word on any of them. So I said to myself, "Who says my dad's a layabout? Who the hell are they to sit and pass judgment", and this little ginger bloke said in his educated way "You may commence" and I thought "To hell with 'em. They can get stuffed." I didn't write a word all morning.

JONES You made no attempt whatsoever?

FRED I did actually. I didn't have the courage of my convictions. Like, this little ginger bloke kept craning round and peering at me sitting there and then he came up leaning on me, mumble, mumble, mumble, and all bad breath. Then he took me outside and began making the point, and he said he'd report me to the Minister of Education or somebody and I thought we'd have the police round again and a delegation of my mum's brothers laying down the law to my dad. So I wrote my name and did one or two sums, but it was eleven o'clock before I done a stroke.

JONES And your dad was disappointed?

FRED No, he never asked me. He knew I'd fail. Like, I went home screwed up to tell him because I never went in for telling lies. But he never asked me. He went and brewed up and he said, "Have a cuppa, Fred", which was something unusual because he usually drained the teapot on his tod. We sat there saying damn all and swigging tea and it was right grand for both of

us—I can't describe it—and he said "Let 'em get stuffed", and I thought about this little educated ginger bloke poncing about in front of his bare blackboards and it was right grand sitting there boozing tea with my dad.
(*silence. Sound of bus running*)

GEORGE They didn't say anything. They just nodded, at first in sympathy and then with the motion of the bus, nodding, nodding, nodding, all the way to the city centre and our Fred didn't seem aware of anybody at all once he'd finished his discourse.
(*bus stops*)

SMITH All right, we're here. Volunteers please to help get this gentleman down the stairs.
(*passengers getting out and going downstairs*)

GEORGE Of course most of them made a mad rush for it but the blokes we had been talking to stayed behind to help and so did the pasty youth whose brother had been among the hooligans the police sorted out on the bus a fortnight ago. He was wearing a striped football topper. Our Fred made a gesture to them meaning thanks but stand clear, and he lifted our dad gently and carried him down the stairs.
(*football crowd in the city centre*)
The problem then was how to get on a bus at all because the football specials fill up rapidly. You have to run to the back of a queue that winds round the town hall. One bus goes and another comes in and it's every man for himself. The four blokes who were helping us stood round in a quandary. You wouldn't believe it but nobody in all those thousands in the city centre took a blind bit of notice.

SMITH Look we can't fight 'em and we can't join 'em. We'd better get a taxi.

FRED The bus is the way he'd expect to go home.
(*pause*)

JONES Hang on. I'll get the inspector.

GEORGE The inspector looked over at us when the man told him, then he went along the line of buses, standing on his tiptoes, shouting in to the drivers. God knows what for, because you'd think it would be simple enough to fill up and drive to the football ground, but I suppose it's what he was paid for and a dozen buses had come and gone before our acquaintance got him over to us.
(*inspector is brisk and jovial*)

INSPECTOR What's your game?

FRED We don't have a game, he's died.

INSPECTOR This is pretty sick stuff, isn't it, taking a corpse to a football match. Are you from Candid Camera?

FRED We want to go home.

INSPECTOR Where's home?

FRED Longshaw Lane.

INSPECTOR Where did you start from?

FRED Home.

INSPECTOR And you're going home? Home from home.

GEORGE Well of course it raised a laugh because we were all thinking of the fretwork motto our dad had splintered over Fred's head and Home, home on the range, like they'd sung, but the inspector took it as a tribute to his comic genius and it cost us nothing to let him go on thinking that.

INSPECTOR Look, lads, I've got my hands full keeping the buses on the move. This isn't a publicity stunt, is it?

FRED Death needs no publicity.

INSPECTOR Where did you start from—not home but this last journey?

FRED The amusement park.

INSPECTOR And it's not publicity?

FRED Look, have you ever lugged your own dad round dead?

INSPECTOR I mean your connection with the amusement park.

SMITH There's confusion here. They were customers at the park, not employees. This gentleman passed on on the ghost train.

INSPECTOR Call an ambulance.

SMITH They don't want an ambulance. They want him to finish in a normal decent way on the bus.

INSPECTOR You should have got the 72X. It'd have dropped you off at the bottom of Longshaw Lane.

FRED We know all that. We don't want to argue the toss about it.

INSPECTOR Are them Red Rovers you've got in your hand? You know you can't use them on the football buses. In any case you'd want to get out at Pole Road, wouldn't you, and the football buses don't stop till they get to the ground.

SMITH Get us a bus and we'll give you a quid.

GEORGE Well, that put the matter in an entirely different light and he was back at the other side of the square shouting on his tiptoes into a cab window and the driver looked across and wrestled with his wheel and the bus pulled out of the line and rolled round empty to where we were standing.

SMITH Quick, get him in.

GEORGE We just made it. There was a hell of an uproar in the crowd and they swarmed across shoving the police horses aside up the town

hall steps, grabbing the rail, pulling their pals on board as the bus gathered speed, leaping some of them and missing and rolling in the road. You'd have thought it was D-Day. And they went on arguing and shouting till the conductor stopped the bus for us at Pole Road. (*bell rings. Bus stops and passengers go quiet. Sound of climbing off*) It was only then when we were getting him down that they realised there was a deceased person on board. The blokes who had helped us got off with us.
(*bus drives off*)

FRED Don't trouble yourself further, you'll miss the match.

SMITH We'll give you a hand, son. I'm only sorry it wasn't done with more decorum.

FRED We'd sooner hump him ourselves if you don't mind. Take his feet, George.

GEORGE Well, they hesitated a bit, then they followed a few yards behind, three middle-aged men in football scarves and the pasty youth in the striped topper. At one stage we stopped for a rest and there was a great explosive roar from the football ground.
(*huge shout of crowd*)
The teams must just have come out. These blokes were obviously a bit wistful about missing it but they didn't show it. They stood at a respectful distance, ready to give us a hand if we wanted it, but our Fred didn't and they just followed up in case. Our Fred stopped short of our door.

FRED I'm wondering how's the best way to put it to her?

GEORGE But he didn't want an answer from me and the blokes realised he didn't want suggestions from them either. He stood holding our dad up against the wall, and you could see how much they looked like each other and our Fred simply didn't know where he was or what to do and we'd have been standing there yet if the brass band man hadn't have stepped forward. Our Fred waved him off and did it himself, not having thought it out, in the worst possible way.
(*Fred knocks on the door which is opened*)

MOTHER Fred, what's happened? What's happened, Fred? Who are these men?

GEORGE They were standing a few yards away and the brass band man gave the pasty youth a dig and glanced at his striped topper. The pasty youth doffed it and held it in front of his chest like a promenade Percy in a Victorian portrait.

MOTHER Fred. Your dad, Fred. What's happened?

FRED He's a goner.

MOTHER But, Fred, I've got his Saturday dinner ready.

FRED Let's get him in. Lift his feet, George.

GEORGE And we got him in and laid him out on the couch and, without thinking, my mum closed the door and we never said thanks to the blokes or offered them a cuppa or even gave the man his quid back.

MOTHER But, Fred, how can he, Fred? I've got his Saturday dinner ready. It's in the oven, roast lamb. I've got his Saturday dinner ready.

GEORGE And she went on and on and the room was bare of ornaments which our dad had flung at Fred and the home home sign that had been a bit of a joke for us was up on the mantelpiece with the mark on the wallpaper behind, and nothing seemed any different from any Saturday. Our Fred could have said something to please her or explain things like he had on the bus. But he didn't. He just sat there like our dad used to do in the happy home as though he didn't care a damn about anything.

FRED All right, mum. There's no point in arguing the toss.

Relics
David Campton

The Cast
Aunt Dorothy

Winifred

Una

Olive

Mrs Parkinson

Relics

Old people are often determined to remain independent and sometimes suffer considerable hardship because of their reluctance to ask for help. Aunt Dorothy was such a person and as she made no direct requests for assistance her relatives didn't go out of their way to see that she was well cared for.

When the play begins, her spirit newly released from its earthly body still lingers in the house where she spent the last years of her life so is in a position to overhear her nieces Una, Winifred and Olive when they arrive to look round after the funeral service.

Although they pretend to be motivated by a sentimental interest in the old lady and her possessions it soon becomes obvious that each is hoping to find some rich pickings and is anxious to stop the others from getting their fair share. To their surprise there seems to be little of value left and they begin to suspect that somebody has stolen a march on them. It is a kindly neighbour, Mrs Parkinson, who explains that over the years the old lady has sold every stick of furniture to provide food and warmth. She mentions, however, that Aunt Dorothy always claimed to have kept her most precious possessions in a small, delicately made box. As soon as she has gone, the nieces try to open it. In desperation, when they can't force the lock, they smash the box to splinters to get at the contents. It contains a few mementoes, precious to Aunt Dorothy but worthless in themselves. They realise that they have destroyed the only remaining thing of value in the house—the box itself.

DOROTHY Help.... Help! (*to herself*) No. One does not call for help. One was brought up to believe in self-reliance. Self-reliance is all that matters in the long run. With self-reliance one does not need to call upon anyone for help.... But in these circumstances.... In what circumstances? In circumstances that lead one to cry help.... Help.... And no one hears. Which is perhaps as well. Help.... One's voice falls dead: the falling dust makes more sound. If only the door and window were not so far away. If only the lace curtains did not proclaim so loudly to the outside world that there is no one in this house in need of help. . . . Help!. . . For what? Are you hungry? No. Are you cold? No. Are you in pain? No. Then why call for help? Because—because I'm alone. . . . Crying for help because you're alone? What next! An old woman must expect to be alone. But one is not sorry for oneself. One has learned to accept. If there is one thing that life teaches, it is how to accept. Age is inevitable if one lives that long. And the older one gets, the more alone one becomes. It's only natural. Nothing to make one cry for. . . . Help? One has been alone before. . . . But never as alone as this. Never so alone that even a mouse would be welcome. Mouse? Mouse. Here, mouse. Hah! There was never more than one mouse here. It invaded the kitchen one baking day, and stood next to the pastry board. Even then one did not call for help. One blow with the rolling-pin, and there was no more left to do than bury the creature in the dustbin.

Bury? Bury. . . . What were those men doing here? There *were* men here. I didn't dream them. Did I? I'm not the sort of old woman who cannot seperate dreams from reality. Dear God, let me not become the sort of woman who cannot seperate dreams from reality. I have my memories, but I know them for memories. The mouse was a memory. Hah! No one else ever knew about the mouse. They might not have fancied the pies. The rolling-pin was scrubbed with soda afterwards, but they might not have cared for pastry rolled with a pin that had struck a mouse dead. Dead?. . . Who were those men? Stiff with artificial sympathy and mock reverence. I've seen them before, or men like them. They come and go and leave nothing but memories behind. But they were not memories. They were real in their black coats and hats. Something has happened here. Something has happened, but I cannot say what. Something. . . . Help!. . . I don't really expect help, but—a little reassurance, perhaps. No! One does not even seek reassurance. One's own assurance is all that one can rely upon. People may not be used as crutches. They sound willing enough. "Lean on me", they say. "Take my arm", they offer. But in the hour of trial where are they? Not here. One is alone and the clock has stopped. One is alone with the falling dust. One. . . . One learns. In the hour of trial one learns to smile and say "No, I don't need anything". "Everything will be all right", one says. One says "Another cup of tea" and "Don't bother, I can wash up afterwards". One remembers the fox and

Spartan boy who died. . . . Who died?

Who were those men who took away a thing of polished elm with brass handles? And if they took away a thing of polished elm with brass handles—why—am I—still—here? Who else was here? Take one from one, and what is left? Help!. . . If only one could talk to someone. But one never did. The habit was lost. One could not talk now—not even to the minister, supposing he should pass this way. Even supposing the minister should pass this way, and pause in this very room, and one surprisingly find the words to ask him—would he know the answer? What was left behind when the men in black took away the thing with brass handles? He might reply "Where your treasure is, there will your heart be also". But one learned that long ago—Luke Six, Verse Twenty-one. "Where your treasure is. . . ." Did one care so much for them? The convex mirror, catching the room in its eye. The petit point fire screen, paid for with time—so many stitches to a minute. The secretaire on which the dust was never allowed to fall. One builds up a rampart of possessions against the time when all else fails. All else has failed. But could they hold one? Surely one is not tied to a secretaire, a convex mirror, a fire screen, the Complete Works of Sir Walter Scott. Can one not let go? After one has accepted everything else, cannot one accept the thing with brass handles? Is one weighed down? Condemned? Earthbound? Help! Help. They took away the thing with brass handles and left me behind. . . . But one does not cry for help—especially when one knows it will not come. . . . Footsteps clatter up and down the street, but they do not stop here. Shadows cross the lace curtains, but they flicker and are gone. The clock has stopped and one is alone. With. . . "Where your treasure is. . ." . . .Shadows pass the lace curtains. Footsteps clatter. Footsteps? Footsteps.

(*Her voice fades away as we hear two pairs of footsteps approaching on bare floorboards*)

UNA The front door shouldn't have been open.

WINIFRED We're here before Olive. That's all we need to bother about.

UNA We had the key.

WINIFRED The key was given to us—officially.

UNA There was no point in collecting the key if the door was open.

WINIFRED We have every right to be here. The undisputed right. Put your suitcase down.

UNA Someone has been careless. We ought to complain.

WINIFRED I remember the old place.

UNA If we don't complain someone may think that *we* have been careless.

WINIFRED But not exactly like this. Not with a bed down here in the front room. I remember a secretaire. At the time I didn't know what a secretaire was, but Aunt Dorothy explained it all to me.

UNA Things may be missing.

WINIFRED There used to be a secretaire against that wall.

UNA *I* don't want to be blamed if it's missing.

WINIFRED And a picture of "Bubbles" hanging over it.

UNA "Cherry Ripe".... I'm going to complain in self-defence.

WINIFRED "Cherry Ripe"?

UNA "Bubbles" is a little boy with bubbles. "Cherry Ripe" is a little girl with cherries. She used to hang over the secretaire.

WINIFRED No secretaire. No little girl. No cherries.

UNA We're not responsible. We didn't leave the door open. We must complain.

WINIFRED I remember that picture perfectly.

UNA Who should we complain to?

WINIFRED Only I remember "Bubbles".

UNA Aunt Ada had "Bubbles" over the meter cupboard. Aunt Dorothy had "Cherry Ripe".

WINIFRED Over the secretaire.

UNA Aunt Ada had "Bubbles".

WINIFRED If Aunt Ada had "Bubbles" it must have gone to....

UNA Oh! You don't think—a certain person....

WINIFRED That certain person doesn't even know that Aunt Dorothy passed on.

UNA Doesn't she?

WINIFRED For once we stole a march on Olive. She wasn't at the funeral. We were given the key.

It might have been the undertakers—forgetting to drop the catch after them. But you'd expect undertakers to know their job better than that.

WINIFRED Can you smell...?

UNA (*with a little shriek*) Gas?

WINIFRED Mothballs.

UNA Mothballs?

WINIFRED The place has been shut up for a fortnight.

UNA You're never going to open the window! We don't want the whole street to know. Word gets around so quickly.

WINIFRED Let it.

UNA I don't like to think of people thinking of us like that.

WINIFRED Like what?

UNA Rummaging.

WINIFRED We're not rummaging. (*she opens the window*)

UNA That's the way they'll think about us. That's the way I should think. I don't want anybody to think I'm rummaging. Especially while I'm doing it. Do come away from the window, Winnie. They'll see you.

WINIFRED They saw us come in. They know we're here. They know why we're here. And personally, I don't give a damn. But if you're feeling sensitive. . . .

UNA I *am* sensitive.

WINIFRED Her clothes. Laid out on the bed.

UNA I saw them.

WINIFRED Give me a hand with them.

UNA I couldn't touch them.

WINIFRED Why not? She died of old age. There's nothing infectious about old age. At least if there is, we're already touched with it. We've all got it coming to us—if we live that long.

UNA You are insensitive, Winifred.

WINIFRED Aunt Dorothy was lucky. She had her full allowance—and some over. Threescore and ten plus. She left these.

UNA (*in a hoarse whisper*) Winnie!

WINIFRED (*not hearing her*) They're good, you know. (*absorbed*) Out of date, but not shoddy. This label alone put fifty-percent on the price. Whenever that was.

UNA (*louder*) Winnie.

WINIFRED A pity I didn't know about this coat sooner: then I could have worn black at the funeral. This style's coming back. Even if it is a bit worn round the button-holes. Of course purple is quite acceptable at a funeral, but you can't beat black.

UNA (*tearfully*) Winn-nee.

WINIFRED Not that I'd ever buy black—not for regular wear. And funerals don't happen all that often.

UNA (*almost screaming*) Winnie!!

WINIFRED What's the matter with you?

UNA Footsteps.

WINIFRED You're hearing things.

UNA You weren't listening.

WINIFRED I've better things to do than to listen for footsteps. And you came along to give me a hand—remember?

UNA A floorboard creaked.

WINIFRED Who's surprised? This is old property. Creak? It's a wonder it isn't falling down.

UNA That creak was on the stairs...well?

WINIFRED Well what?

UNA Well.

WINIFRED (*shouting*) You out there. You can come out. (*there is no response*) We know you're out there. (*silence*) There's no reply.

UNA If I were out there, I shouldn't reply.

WINIFRED Any other bright ideas?

UNA Well, if I were you, I'd look through the other rooms.

OLIVE (*coming into the room suddenly*) It won't do any good.

UNA (*shrieks*)

OLIVE The other rooms are empty.

WINIFRED Olive!

UNA (*groans*)

OLIVE Hullo, Winnie.

WINIFRED You half-killed Una.

UNA The doctor warned me against shocks. "No shocks, Mrs Waring", he said. Shocks are absolutely forbidden. A tap on the shoulder could prove fatal.

OLIVE I'll bear that in mind.

WINIFRED You weren't at the funeral.

OLIVE No.

WINIFRED She was your aunt, too, you know.

OLIVE Yes.

WINIFRED I see you brought a suitcase.

OLIVE Yes.

WINIFRED Had a good look round, no doubt.

OLIVE Yes.

WINIFRED Trust you to be first.

OLIVE Yes.

WINIFRED Well, Una and I are here now, you notice.

OLIVE Yes.

WINIFRED From now on everything will be straightforward and above board. . . . Una, would you mind carrying your own weight?

UNA I'd as soon recommend poison as a shock to a woman in your condition, he told me. "You've nerves like piano wires", he said.

WINIFRED We'll go through the rooms together.

OLIVE I told you—the other rooms are empty. Except for curtains at the front—to keep up appearances.

WINIFRED Do you expect us to believe that?

OLIVE No.

WINIFRED I wasn't born yesterday.

OLIVE No.

WINIFRED Olive Prendergast, it's over twenty years since we last met, and I don't think any better of you now than I did then.

OLIVE No?

WINIFRED I'm going upstairs.

UNA I'll come with you.

WINIFRED You'll stay here.

UNA With her?

WINIFRED She could have that suitcase packed, and be half-way to King's Cross before I'm down again. You'll keep your eyes open. And I'll tell you something else, Olive Prendergast. . . .

OLIVE It's Turner now. Mrs Edward Turner. Has been for fifteen years. Didn't we send you a piece of cake?

WINIFRED If you want to throw dust in my eyes, you've got to get up early in the morning.

OLIVE I did.

WINIFRED All empty indeed.

OLIVE Didn't you wonder what a chest of drawers was doing down here? There used to be a secretaire against that wall.

WINIFRED With a picture of "Bubbles" over it.

OLIVE & UNA "Cherry Ripe".

WINIFRED (walking away) You just keep your eyes open, our Una.

UNA You laid these clothes out on the bed.

OLIVE And you've sorted through them again.

UNA No, it was Winnie who . . . (suddenly realises what she is saying) She had every right.

OLIVE Of course.

UNA We're the only surviving relations—you, me, and Winnie.

OLIVE That's so.

UNA So we're quite entitled. . . .

OLIVE Help yourself. That coat's not my style.

UNA We were given the key. We certainly didn't expect to find you.

OLIVE You meant to be first.

UNA Yes. I mean—you were unexpected.

OLIVE I wasn't supposed to know.

UNA Yes. I mean no. I mean . . . . You always did have a nasty way of twisting one's words. I mean—you're here.

OLIVE And just as eager to get my feet in the trough as you.

UNA There. You see? . . . Really!

OLIVE There's only one difference between us. I can take a joke.

UNA This is not an occasion for joking. Poor Aunt Dorothy.

OLIVE What can you remember of her? A nose. A long, thin, cold, nose, slightly red at the tip, that got in the way when she kissed you. That's all I remember.

UNA I can remember the smell of peppermint. Winnie believes it was mothballs, but I'm sure it was peppermint.

OLIVE I remember a nose. It isn't much to leave behind. A smell of peppermint, and a nose.

UNA She left much more than that.

OLIVE Here comes Winnie again, clattering down the stairs. No carpet on the stairs. Can Winnie take a joke?
(*Winnie approaches, panting*)

WINIFRED They're empty. All empty.

OLIVE I did find a piece of dry soap in the bathroom.

WINIFRED They've been stripped. Not a stick. Not a stitch.

UNA Upstairs?

WINIFRED Everywhere. It's desecration.

OLIVE Not desecration, Winnie. Property isn't holy. Desirable, but not holy. And Aunt Dorothy was no saint.

WINIFRED She had money. We know that.

OLIVE Had. That's what we've been. Had.

WINIFRED Property has been removed without our knowledge or consent.

UNA We ought to complain.

WINIFRED Well everything's going back. I know my rights. Whatever you took from those rooms is going back.

OLIVE Dust on my shoes. But you raised as much. Let's count our share of the dust as equal.

UNA The police ought to be told.

OLIVE No.

WINIFRED Scared? What became of "Cherry Ripe"?

OLIVE That's a thought. Somebody actually paid good money for it.

WINIFRED Well, who was it?

OLIVE Yes, indeed. Who'd want "Cherry Ripe"? Incredible.

WINIFRED You sold it.

OLIVE I did?

WINIFRED Somebody did. With all the rest. And you don't want the police called in.

OLIVE What are the police going to see? Three vultures squabbling over dry bones. Let's keep our humiliation to ourselves.

MRS PARKINSON (*outside*) Anybody there?

OLIVE If we can.

MRS PARKINSON (*outside*) Hullo?

WINIFRED Did you leave the front door open?

UNA It *was* open.

WINIFRED Now we'll have half the street in.

₂S PARKINSON (*approaching*) There you are. I'd been keeping an eye open, but I was down at the shops after all. That's life, isn't it? You'll be the nieces, won't you?

WINIFRED Mrs Beedle and Mrs Waring.

OLIVE Mrs Turner.

₂S PARKINSON I'm Mrs Parkinson from next door. Mrs Wilkinson said you must be the nieces when she saw you bringing the suitcases.

WINIFRED We didn't hear you knock.

₂S PARKINSON I got used to popping in to make sure she was all right. She shouldn't have been on her own at her age, but she was independent. "Time enough to be looked after when I can't look after myself," she said.

UNA Did she?

₂S PARKINSON But that never happened. Went off in her sleep. A lovely way to go. I found her, you know—just popped in for a peek at her, and there she was—gone.

WINIFRED You popped in.

₂S PARKINSON I was popping in and out all the time. A bowl of soup here. A slice of toast there. "I've made too much for Wilfred and me," I'd say. "Be a love and finish it up or it'll be thrown away." She'd take it then as a favour to me. It had to be put as a favour to me, you understand. She'd never accept a favour from anybody. She had standards.

OLIVE Some of us do.

WINIFRED (*heavy with meaning*) So you'd know where everything was.

PARKINSON I thought some little thing to remind me.... "They'll never object," I said to Wilfred. "What you've never had you never miss." Some knick-knack. It's not the value it's the sentiment. Like—er.... Or—er.... I'm sure she'd have wanted.... Just a.... To be remembered, you see. Maybe.... The fact is, there isn't anything worth taking.

OLIVE We had noticed.

WINIFRED (*accusingly*) Where did it all go?

PARKINSON Go?

WINIFRED The musical box.

UNA The convex mirrors.

WINIFRED The fire-screen.

UNA The Complete Works of Sir Walter Scott.

WINIFRED Cherry Ripe.

OLIVE The secretaire.

MRS PARKINSON Now you are taking me back. I can just remember the secretaire going.

WINIFRED Where?

MRS PARKINSON To the auctioneers, of course. We hadn't long moved in when we noticed that being moved out. I told Wilfred to lend a hand, but it wasn't needed. The removal men knew what they were about. It was an expensive piece. She said it took up too much room and harboured dust. I could see her point of view. The valuable pieces went first.

OLIVE To the auctioneers?

MRS PARKINSON Then the rest, bit by bit. I suppose nobody would have what's left. Even the second-hand trade can be choosey. When we tried to part with our old three-piece do you think we could sell it? We had to pay the dustman in the end. That's life, isn't it? I did think this ornament, but....

OLIVE I'm sure my cousins won't object.

MRS PARKINSON (*disappointed*) It's been mended in two places.

WINIFRED She sold everything?

MRS PARKINSON She had to live.

WINIFRED It all went?

MRS PARKINSON I suggested letting rooms. "Nobody would think the worse for letting in this day and age", I told her. But she had those standards.

OLIVE It still happens.

MRS PARKINSON If she let rooms, people might think that she was in need, and she wouldn't have anybody think that. Whenever a self-denying envelope came through the door, she always put something in. A brave old soul. Even if a bit obstinate. Well—it's been a pleasure....

WINIFRED All—sold.

OLIVE I wonder what a wild goose looks like.

WINIFRED Eh?

OLIVE We've been chasing one.

MRS PARKINSON You've found the box, of course.

UNA The box?

MRS PARKINSON I never saw what was in it because she kept it locked. Once I came in a bit sudden like and she slammed the lid shut. Rather short she was that day. She always took great care of the box.

WINIFRED Oh, that box. Yes, yes.

UNA What box?

WINIFRED *The* box.

MRS PARKINSON You know about the box, then.

WINIFRED We've got it in hand.

S PARKINSON I thought I ought to mention it. I wouldn't want you to pass it over as of no account.

OLIVE There's no danger.

S PARKINSON Thank you for the.... (*walking away*) It'll remind me.

WINIFRED Una, drop the catch on that front door, after her.

UNA A box.

WINIFRED And if there's a bolt, push it home.

UNA We haven't found a box.

WINIFRED We're going to. And we don't want to be disturbed again, do we?

UNA (*walking away*). I'd better shut the front door.

WINIFRED You can see it all now, can't you?

OLIVE No.

WINIFRED She had money.

OLIVE It was said.

WINIFRED They get like that, you know. They want it in their hands.

OLIVE Do they?

WINIFRED They want the money where they can count it.

OLIVE If they've got it.

UNA (*coming back*) There were two bolts and a chain.

WINIFRED Banks are no good. They've got to feel it between their fingers.

UNA Feel what?

WINIFRED They know they can't take it with them, but they try. They keep it by them to the end. She did.

OLIVE Did she?

UNA What are you talking about.

WINIFRED The box. The box Aunt Dorothy kept all her money in.

OLIVE In theory.

WINIFRED Can you doubt it?

OLIVE I doubt everything 'til I see it.

WINIFRED Don't you understand? That's why everything was sold—to convert it into money. That's why there's nothing in the bank. It's all in hard cash.

UNA In a box?

WINIFRED The old miser.

OLIVE A bit lumpy to sleep on, don't you think?

WINIFRED She knew what she was doing. Don't stand about, Una, Strip the bed.

OLIVE Hope springs eternal.

WINIFRED You're not doing much to help.

A drawer is pulled out.

OLIVE I'm enjoying myself in my own way.

WINIFRED Underclothes. Not many either.

OLIVE Do you think she sold the rest?

A drawer is pulled out.

WINIFRED This drawer's empty.

OLIVE It might be jammed at the back.

WINIFRED Ah-ha!

The drawer is pulled out and it falls on the floor with a bang.

UNA *(a shriek)*

WINIFRED It isn't.

UNA You know what shocks do to me.

OLIVE Think twice before you find the money. Your heart might not take the strain.

UNA It isn't in the bed. It isn't under the bed.

OLIVE Under the carpet?

WINIFRED There isn't a carpet.

OLIVE Under the floorboards?

WINIFRED You can laugh.

OLIVE I know.

WINIFRED It's your money as well as ours. She kept it here.

OLIVE She kept something. Her dignity.

WINIFRED What's dignity?

OLIVE I lost mine for a while. I'm trying to recover it. She had standards. Will you go shares in them?

UNA Winnie! The chest of drawers.

WINIFRED I've just been through it.

UNA Not in. On top. With a lace doyley and a photograph on top.

WINIFRED Ah!

OLIVE *(taken aback)* So there *was* a box.

UNA Where anybody could see it.

WINIFRED Cunning. Cunning. She knew the best place to hide it.

UNA It's a pretty box.

OLIVE Expensive.

UNA Worth six pounds, do you think?

OLIVE Nine, perhaps.

WINIFRED Maybe twelve.

OLIVE Or even fifteen.

UNA Twenty-one?

WINIFRED I shouldn't wonder.

OLIVE But she kept it.

UNA To hoard her treasure in.

WINIFRED What better? This is the box. This. Only it's locked.

OLIVE Let me try.

WINIFRED Can't wait to get your hands on it now, can you?

OLIVE There must be a key somewhere. On the mantlepiece.

UNA In the bed.

WINIFRED Where...?

UNA What about...?

OLIVE No.

WINIFRED Or...

OLIVE Yes?

UNA No...perhaps...

WINIFRED That's right.

OLIVE No.... Ah!

UNA What?

WINIFRED No.

A rattle of a knife on the box.

UNA You never used to be so slow getting into my money box.

OLIVE If you don't want me to help....

WINIFRED It's not that sort of box. We could have a key made.

OLIVE And who holds the box meanwhile?

WINIFRED I'll have to take it away.

OLIVE Will you? And who'll be present when you open up?

WINIFRED If the box can't be opened....

OLIVE Break it.

UNA But it's such a pretty box. Expensive, you said. Twenty-one pounds would be seven pounds each. Enough to cover our expenses.

OLIVE Is it more valuable than what's inside? Pass me that poker.

UNA It's a shame.

OLIVE You don't have to watch.

She hits the box with the poker.

UNA Oh. Oh. Oh. Oh. Oh. Oh. Oh. Oh.

The box splinters open.

UNA Ah!

WINIFRED There!

An expectant pause.

OLIVE Thousands?

UNA A doll.

WINIFRED It was hers.

UNA When she was a girl. She told me so.

OLIVE She let me hold it once. Not for long. She didn't trust children. They break things.

WINIFRED The moths have been at it.... A pipe.

OLIVE Uncle Arthur's.

WINIFRED I don't remember him.

OLIVE Nobody does.

UNA He was our uncle.

OLIVE This is a pretty little box.

WINIFRED It's not valuable.

OLIVE No. Not valuable. Just a pretty little box. It rattles.

WINIFRED Is it—?

UNA It might be.

OLIVE Do you think it is?

WINIFRED There's nothing else valuable.

UNA It's a box inside a box. It ought to be precious.

OLIVE You open it, then. I refuse to harbour any more expectations. I've lowered my standards enough for one day.

UNA Let me have it then. Let me. (*gives a shriek*) That was a mean trick to play.

OLIVE What was it?

UNA You know all about my heart.

WINIFRED Here it is. It's a tooth.

OLIVE A tooth?

WINIFRED A baby tooth.

OLIVE We had a cousin Adrian.

UNA Adrian?

OLIVE Before your time. He was drowned in the canal when he was six.

WINIFRED A baby tooth.

OLIVE Anything else?

WINIFRED A silver bell off a wedding cake. An invitation to something. It says "Please come to my seventh birthday party".

OLIVE Oh, no. That's rubbing it in too hard.

WINIFRED A birthday card. A key.

OLIVE It won't fit anything.

WINIFRED I suppose not. Where are you going?

OLIVE Home. You can give my share to Oxfam.

UNA The box was the only thing worth taking.

OLIVE We broke that.

WINIFRED Half a minute. I'll come with you. Una?

UNA She didn't have much at the end.

OLIVE Only her standards. We couldn't share them, even if we wanted to.

UNA The doll. Is it worth taking the doll?

OLIVE Moths get at everything.

They shut the door behind them.

AUNT DOROTHY (*as their footsteps fade*) They've gone. Gone. With the secretaire,

the mirror, the fire-screen and The Complete Works. All gone.
Except... Adrian? Arthur? Ah!
She gives a long contented sigh that fades as the play ends.

Jump!
Ken Whitmore

The Cast
Aunt

Uncle

Frederick

A Mole

Mr Morrisarde

Harold Harridge

Sir Peter

Hoskins

Station Announcer

Compere

A Male Panellist

A Female Panellist

Gumbolt

The Blue-Suited Ruler

The Fur-Hatted Ruler

Jump!

Sometimes it seems that most of the problems facing mankind would be solved easily if only people could be persuaded to use their energies in working together. This story is about one boy's attempt to get everybody in the world to act in unison.

Frederick, born and bred in the country, lives on a farm with his uncle and aunt, two down-to-earth people whose lives don't allow much time for anything beyond the practical concerns of the moment. It is one of his tasks to deliver the milk to Professor Morrisarde who lives at the top of a steep crag not far from the farm. On the journey his dog, Joy, attracts his attention to a hole in the ground where he discovers a mole who tells him that the earth's crust has been so weakened by mankind that it is in imminent danger of collapse. Unless something is done quickly, he says, there will be an earthquake which will destroy London and within a week the whole of the earth's crust will break up. When Frederick asks what he can do about it the mole's answer is simple: he must spread the news quickly and tell all the people in the world to jump in the air at the same time. During the few seconds when everybody is aloft, the moles will prop up the earth's crust and the world will be made safe.

Although Professor Morrisarde believes Frederick, he doesn't find it easy to convince other people. Even when the first prophecy comes true and London is reduced to a heap of rubble the world's leaders still can't agree about the measures to be taken. It is only when Gumbolt, the wise ruler of the moles, intervenes that the ordinary people are able to sink their differences to work together for the common good.

Unlike the other plays in this volume, *Jump!* is a fable. Its apparent simplicity is deceptive and the story is capable of more than one interpretation.

The farmhouse where Frederick lives with his aunt and uncle. The family are having breakfast.

AUNT Get stuck into that porridge, Frederick. Being fat's nowt to send you to jail for that I knows on.

FREDERICK Honest, Auntie, I've got no appetite.

UNCLE Come on—trench into it. It'll stick to your ribs.

AUNT You don't set him to enough work. Lads nowadays don't know what work means. When I was a lass we'd all to buzz round like bees, I can tell you.

UNCLE Aye, us young 'uns had to spin round. I were glad of night.

FREDERICK I milked the house cow this morning, Auntie. An' I mucked out the horses' paddock.

UNCLE Aye, and I saw you watching the new lambs jumping. You were putting down roots. Lads these days are as lazy as the dog as laid its head agin' t'wall to bark.

UNCLE (*eating*) All right, let him alone. He earns his keep.

FREDERICK Uncle, could I take the old man his milk the long way round this morning? Just this once?

UNCLE Oh, now we're getting at the truth. It's that what's put you off your corn, is it?

FREDERICK It makes my legs wobble just to think about it, Uncle. Couldn't I walk round the village and up the hill the gentle way?

UNCLE (*scornful*) Gentle? Talk like a big wench and your Aunt'll put you in petticoats. You want to walk three miles round when we can see the smoke from his chimney from here? It's the climb still scares you, is it?

FREDERICK It scares our teacher—and he's a mountaineer.

UNCLE (*laughing*) Mountaineer?

FREDERICK He is! The scar's a sheer face, he says. He won't believe I go up it every day. And I get vertigo.

UNCLE Vertigo, indigo, Abednigo! None of your foreign tongues.
The chair scrapes as he gets up from the breakfast table.
Come here, Frederick. Come to the window.

FREDERICK (*going away towards the window*) Aye, Uncle Makepeace?

UNCLE There she is. Just behold that scar. Look up yonder. What d'you see?

FREDERICK A crow flapping. Curlews and peewits. Primroses running up to the bracken.

UNCLE Nay. Right up near the top. Little specks of white.

FREDERICK Lambs.

UNCLE Lambs as old as this morning's violets. Jumping up and kicking their heels out on ledges no thicker than a cricket bat. Are you as brave as a lamb, Frederick?

FREDERICK I get giddy. My head goes round. My hands won't grip.

AUNT Hands won't grip! Your Uncle's only tutoring you to be a manly man like your Dad. There was a man for you. Never mind your mountaineers. He were never seen to blink.

UNCLE Scared of nowt. Makepeace, he says to me when he were eight, learn me to swim. So we go to the Wharfe at Linton Falls, and it's in flood, right deep and strong. Noo then, he says, shove me in the watter. (*pause*) And he swam.

FREDERICK None of the village lads dares climb the scar.

UNCLE I could carve better lads out of a bunch of bananas.

FREDERICK Why did they want to go and build a house up there anyroad with the wind screaming and howling right away from the world?

AUNT The monks built Scar Top in the dark centuries. They had a lot of thinking to do.

UNCLE And they could watch their flocks, like.

FREDERICK Mr Morrisarde's no monk. And he's got no sheep but them as hop over his wall. What's he doing up there? Where's he from?

UNCLE If tha doesn't know, it's a poor look-out for other folk. Nobody but you hardly sees him. He's an off-comer and he keeps himself close. Now clear off and take him his milk.

AUNT I've topped his can up with good thick cream, tell him.
We hear the clink of the milk can as it is handed to Frederick.
Here lad, take the can. Hook it over your wrist and make sure that lid's tight on. And don't wobble o'er much on the way up or you'll have it spilling all out. And take your daft hound with you.

FREDERICK Uncle, it's only this once....

UNCLE (*cutting him short*) No! Now clear out.

FREDERICK All right, Uncle.

UNCLE Get tha gone, thou bletherhead. Shift thisel'.
Frederick opens the door.

FREDERICK (*whistling to dog*) Come on, Joy! Come on then, girl!
The door closes and we are in the open with birdsong and sheep.
Come on, Joy, I'll race you over the bridge.
We hear his feet running over the grass.
Hey! You big cheat! Over the bridge, I said!
The dog splashes into the river.
I didn't say swim the beck. You'll not get me in there. It's icy from the fell tops. (*pause*) I bet I can get to the far bank first!
He runs through the grass then stops at a bridge.
(*panting*) Come on, you daft wench! I won you. Sheep dogs are supposed to be clever. What's matter, has watter paralysed thee? (*to himself*) She's as much brain as a coconut.
Splashing as the dog scrambles from water.

FREDERICK Come on out. Hey! Don't shake water all over me you giddy

beggar. Get down! Down! (*pause*) Hark.
Repeated call of a cuckoo.
He never gets fed up hearing himself, the bletherhead. (*calling*)
Joy! Come back here!
The dog barks in the distance
(*to himself*) She climbs the scar three times while I'm climbing it
once. (*pause*) I could run away and live in a town. (*pause*) Nay,
crushed wi' crowds and rows on rows o' streets. I want a big
stretch of sky aw round me. I want to skid a stone in a beck...
here's one...like (*he grunts*) that!
Three plops as the stone skids on the surface of the river.
A three-er!
Excited barking of the dog in the distance.
What's she found now? Tail goin' like a windscreen wiper.
He climbs uphill through crunching bracken.
Joy, girl!
The dog barks excitedly nearby
(*approaching*) Come away, girl! What have you found? Hey,
away from that hole. You want your head stuck down it?
Worried whining from the dog.

MOLE   (*his voice is close but muffled, he is talking from down a hole*) Boy!

FREDERICK Who were that?

MOLE   (*shouting*) Boy! Get that blasted animal out of here!

FREDERICK She's skedaddled. She's hid behind that old mountain ash,
mister. You've scared her witless. Where are you, mister?

MOLE   Come closer, boy. (*pause*) The hole, confound it! Kneel down and
look in my hole.
Pause.

FREDERICK (*close*) Are you down there, mister?

MOLE   There you are. Isn't it a grand day? But there were a good drop
of rain in the night. Fair stirred the becks.

FREDERICK (*astonished*) You're a mole!

MOLE   Aye, listen. I'm sorry if I were a bit on the rude side but I can't
abide a dog. There's a lot of fox in a dog and for a mole there's
nothing more terrible than a fox. Barring a Spudkins, of course.

FREDERICK (*surprised*) A Spudkins?

MOLE   Don't say you've never heard of Spudkins. The name Spudkins,
Mole Catcher, is a byword for beastliness in these parts. Genera-
tions of 'em, right down from Oliver Cromwell. Don't make out
you've never heard of Spudkins.

FREDERICK (*in confusion*) Well...I don't rightly know what....

MOLE   The boy's blushing. You're blushing, boy. (*pause*) Oh God and

76

Gumbolt, you're not... You can't be ...

FREDERICK (*ashamed*) Yes.

MOLE A Spudkins!

FREDERICK Aye.

MOLE What manner of Spudkins might you be? Which branch?

FREDERICK I live with my Uncle Makepeace.

MOLE (*in a squeal*) Makepeace Spudkins?

FREDERICK Yes. (*pause*) Well—so long.

MOLE (*quickly*) No! Wait. (*slyly*) Will you do an old mole a favour? Will you just put your hand down this hole?

FREDERICK Uncle Makepeace says a mole can give a sharp nip if you're not careful.

MOLE (*wistful*) Old Mole Gumbolt taught him that in 1937. He took his finger clean off. It was as sweet as a baby lark. (*pause*) Just put your hand inside here.

FREDERICK D'you think I'm daft or summat?

MOLE There's no trust left upstairs. I don't know why we went on saving it.

FREDERICK Saving what?

MOLE Stopping it crumpling like a paper bag that goes *bang*. But it's too late now. We moles can't do any more. It's had it.

FREDERICK Eh? What's had it?

MOLE (*grumpily*) None of your business. I'll bid you good morning.

FREDERICK Hey, no, hang on. Go on, tell us.

MOLE You wouldn't take the word of a mole. You don't trust me.

FREDERICK Well...I think I do.

MOLE Good. Just put your hand inside here.

FREDERICK I don't like the way you say that. Your teeth kind of rasp and I think you're slobbering.

MOLE Shlobbering!

FREDERICK There—see?

MOLE I must admit I am salivating slightly but that's only because it's coming up to nine o'clock. We feed at intervals of three hours, you know, at the chiming hours. Nine-twelve-three, and sho on. So on, confound it! We salivate in order to digest our food more easily, to shoften it up. Think of eating unsoftened wireworms or leatherjackets.

FREDERICK Or baby larks.

MOLE (*offended*) There...I see you'll never trust me. Be off with you and enjoy yourself while there's still time, because it's later than you think, my lad. And keep away from London next Friday.

FREDERICK Eh?

MOLE I'll be seeing you.

FREDERICK No, wait.

MOLE (*going*) Toodle-pip.

FREDERICK (*quickly*) I'm putting my hand in.

MOLE (*close*) Where? I don't see it.

FREDERICK Moles can't see.

MOLE Can't they, though? It was old Shakespeare put that slander about. "Tread softly that the blind mole may not hear a footfall," he said. The blithering fool. Some moles have keener sight than a kestrel. Old Mole Gumbolt, when he were a young buck, could see a hole in a ladder. Now get that hand put in sharp!

FREDERICK (*in some fear*) Here it comes. No biting!

MOLE (*after a pause, sniffing in a puzzled way*) What's this?

FREDERICK (*giggling*) You're tickling me finger.

MOLE What did you say they called you, boy?

FREDERICK Spudkins. Frederick Spudkins.

MOLE Are you sure?

FREDERICK Frederick Kitchener Spudkins.

MOLE That's right queer.

FREDERICK Eh?

MOLE This is no Spudkins. A Spudkins is stringy and strychnine-tasting. A Spudkins is bony and proddy. (*pause*) Did you say *Kitchener* Spudkins?

FREDERICK That were my father's name. Trooper Frederick Kitchener. Killed in action. Military medal and Bar. I've got it at home in a box lined wi' plum velvet. And my mother died when I were three. So then I went to live with her sister, Aunt Matilda, Uncle Makepeace's wife. And he gi' me his name, Spudkins.

MOLE (*angrily*) Well you shouldn't have took it! (*pause*) By, that were a close shave! If you'd a been a Spudkins I'd have had your finger off wi' good speed. Oh, I know I gave my word, but what's a promise to a human? What's trust up in the sunlight? Stoop as low as you like to spite a Spudkins. But a Kitchener's never harmed a mole. Now take that hand away before I'm tempted.

FREDERICK There. It's out. (*pause*) Now tell us. What's had it? And why should I give London a miss come Friday?

MOLE Well. Just put your lugs to t'hoil and hearken, Frederick. That's right. It's a long tale so let's tunnel right through the the hill and never mind the footways. (*pause*) It's old earth herself that's had it, Frederick.

FREDERICK Old earth?

MOLE Look about you at the dips and rises in the land—the brown fells and the bright valleys, the aching greens. What's it call to mind? It's like a bedcover over an untidy sleeper—a man lying on his belly wi' his rump i' the air. Have a good deep gaze. Can you spy an elbow and an armpit and a finger or two? And them gurt bulging buttocks?

FREDERICK *(in a voice of wonder)* Aye.

MOLE There's sheep and cattle scattered over that bedcover and people with their silos and double deckers and concrete mixers. All of 'em taking it for gospel the ground's solid under their clog soles. Not knowing owt about that sleeper down below.

FREDERICK Nay, but there ent any sleeper.

MOLE That's what I'm tunnelling towards! There is a sleeper, lad, and that's the trouble. And comes the time he scratches an elbow or wags a toe the mountains break like china bowls. His name's Magma and his bedcover's twenty mile thick—the earth's crust.

FREDERICK Nay!

MOLE He only had to twitch an eyelid under the Shen-Si Province in China...in 1556 that were...and 83,000 people were swallowed up wi' their pigs and pagodas and paper dragons. *(pause)* They were given fair warning but not a soul among 'em jumped.

FREDERICK Jumped?

MOLE Jumped. If only they'd all jumped in the air they'd have given us time. And what's a little jump in exchange for life rolling sweetly on?

FREDERICK You mean—everybody in China should 'a' jumped?

MOLE Look at it this way. You've got your bedcover—old earth's crust. The sleeper turns and what happens? The cover sinks in some parts and rises in others. You've slept in a bed. You must know that.

FREDERICK Aye, but...

MOLE Wait a bit. Listen. What if there's somebody else under the bedcover, besides the sleeper, to make sure it keeps still whatever happens? To prop it up? To maintain the equilibrium, the status quo? Frederick, lad, there is somebody down there to prop it up. Somebody down there under the earth's crust. Leastwise, some bodies. Seventy million and seven, if you want to be fussy. Moles.

FREDERICK Nay!

MOLE The sleeper turns and by all the laws of God and gravity the bedcover sinks and tosses. *(pause)* But we don't let it. At the smallest stirring of the sleeper we spring to our posts—digging and delving, shoring and shelving.

FREDERICK You what?

79

MOLE Dragging and hauling and pushing and heaving. Deep down in the true dark. A masterpiece of engineering by seventy million and seven moles of one mind. And up above a blade of grass wouldn't wave to tell you what was happening under its roots.

FREDERICK I still don't see where jumping comes into it.

MOLE Too many people up on top. Think of that great load of people pressing down from above! Four thousand million people on this planet—pressing down, pressing down. So any gap between the bedcover and the sleeper's filled in a flash and packed down tight like snow stamped down by a foot on a flagstone. A weight like that's too much even for the moles. We're flattened and fossilised between the rocky layers. Turned to mole coal in the blink of an eye. Now. If that pressure could be relieved...just for as long as it takes to blink...we could get the job done. We're that fast. And relieving the pressure for that long's as easy as blinking. All it needs is for the people above to....

FREDERICK Jump?

MOLE With one accord. And while they were in mid-air we'd finish the stabilising. (*pause*) But nobody's ever jumped. Nobody jumped in Shen-Si. Nobody jumped in the Sunken Land of Bus, or the Lost Continent of Mu. That's why they are sunken and why they are lost.

FREDERICK Nay, but you couldn't expect folk to jump if nobody told 'em.

MOLE But somebody did. We always do. In Shen-Si it was a girl named Weng Lak Sang. She ran to tell the Mandarins and princes but they preferred to die with their precious incredulity intact. Man's strongest faith is in his own capacity for disbelief, Frederick. It'll be the downfall of London on Friday and the end of civilisation the Friday after. June the tenth.

FREDERICK Aye, but why?

MOLE The sleeper's waking up. For century heaped on century he slept in peace. Oh, he gave a twitch and capsized a Mu or an Atlantis every few thousand year, but mostly he slept like a bairn. But now he's rousing himself. Who sleeps easy when his bloodstream's filled wi' poison? Who lies gentle when jumping jacks and thunderbolts are going off around his lugs? It's all man's wickedness with his underground fireworks and his dying of the rivers sky blue pink. Is it any wonder old Magma's running a fever? We've been keeping him under observation and there's no doubt. He's going to throw up his left arm on Friday. And his left arm lies directly under London.

FREDERICK (*whispering*) Get off! (*pause*) And what about the Friday after that?

MOLE On that day—at ten past three in the afternoon—Magma will jump up with a terrible cry and fling off his bedcover—just as if a cockroach had run up his pyjamas. And the earth's crust'll go whizzing through the universe as it might be the skin off a rice pudding.

FREDERICK (*with wonder*) I pictures it. (*pause*) But I thought you said you always warned 'em. Has London been warned?

MOLE We told a man named Harold Harridge. He was strolling along the banks of the Thames at Greenwich at eleven in the morning, knocking the heads off daffodils with his walking stick.

FREDERICK When a mowdie spoke to him?

MOLE Just like I spoke to you.

FREDERICK What did he do?

MOLE Harold Harridge just stood there, chewing his moustache with his eyes growing bigger and rounder...then he dropped his stick and ran off with his knees raised very high.

FREDERICK (*to himself*) You could carve a better man out of a banana. (*pause*) And...and what about the rest of the world? Has anybody been warned about that?

MOLE Why, of course, lad. Naturally. What d'you think we are— *spurious* moles?
Pause.

FREDERICK Who?

MOLE Who what?

FREDERICK Did you warn about t'world?

MOLE Frederick Kitchener Spudkins.

FREDERICK (*after a pause, horrified*) Me? What can I do about it?

MOLE There's no call for long faces. Just make sure everybody in the world jumps and the moles'll do the rest. Now get thee off home.

FREDERICK (*dazed*) I...I mun climb the scar first...the old man's milk.

MOLE Does that scare thee?

FREDERICK You'd want nerves like park railings.

MOLE Aye, well. So long, old lad. (*going*) So long.
Frederick whistles and shouts the dog.

FREDERICK Come on, girl. Out from behind that tree. He's gone. (*to himself*) If he were ever there. (*to the dog*) Come on! Up that scar!
The wind rages as Frederick climbs the scar. His boots scrambling on the rock.
(*panting, as he climbs*) Make...all...the people...jump. All the folk...in...the world.
Silence. Then fade in the sound of a strong wind on the moor at the top of

the scar.

Leave them sheep be, or I'll leather thee! (*to himself*) For a man to live up here where the scar touches the sky and the moor starts rollin' up to nowhere, he'd have to be tapped.

He knocks on the door of Mr Morrisarde's house.

One day this house'll just take off and blow away like them peewits.

The door opens.

MORRISARDE Ah, the milk boy.

FREDERICK Mr Morrisarde, I think a mole just spoke to me.

MORRISARDE (*pause*) Come in out of the wind.

Fade out.

Frederick's bedroom.

AUNT Frederick! Wake up, Frederick Spudkins!

The bed creaks as he turns over.

FREDERICK Eh? What's the time?

AUNT One hint's enough for a wise man. Now out of that bed sharp. And put your best flowered shirt and tie on. They're on the dresser.

FREDERICK It ent Sunday, is it?

AUNT Nay, Monday. I can't make out what you've told the old one, Mr Morrisarde, but he's downstairs wi' a suitcase and Thompson's cab. Don't say owt but he's wearin' his bedroom slippers. You're goin' to London on the train. There's a few screws loose this morning.

Fade out.

The kitchen.

Uncle is talking to Mr Morrisarde as he munches his breakfast.

UNCLE He's not an untruthful child, Mr Morrisarde. He's as innocent as a pot dog. But I know everything about moles and they don't talk.

MORRISARDE The world believes they can't take off a finger, Mr Spudkins.

UNCLE Aye...well, a mole made me a present o' this stump, I'll a'warrant.

AUNT Eat up, Makepeace, it's not the end of the world.

MORRISARDE It was the quotation from Shakespeare that convinced me. Then there was the use of that recondite word Magma. And then Mr Harold Harridge.

AUNT I don't rightly see how it calls for you two to go traipsing off to London.

MORRISARDE Because London will be the epicentre of an earthquake. The point of maximum intensity. And later the whole world will be destroyed.

UNCLE It wouldn't suit.

AUNT And what can you and our Frederick do about it?

MORRISARDE We can try to see that everybody in the world jumps in the air at the same time.

AUNT (*pause*) 'Appen.
Fade out.

The railway station.

ANNOUNCER (*over loudspeaker*) The train at platform 2 is the 8.15 . . . calling at Leeds, Wakefield, Doncaster, Grantham and London King's Cross.
Fade out.

A street in London.

Mr Morrisarde knocks at the front door of Harold Harridge's house. It opens.

HARRIDGE Yes? Can I help you?

MORRISARDE This young man and I are looking for Mr Harold Harridge.

HARRIDGE That is me, sir.

MORRISARDE It's about your conversation with a mole at Greenwich.

HARRIDGE Oh!
His body thumps to the floor.

FREDERICK He's dropped down dead!

MORRISARDE (*calmly*) He's just fainted, Frederick.
Fade out.

Inside the house.

MORRISARDE Would you like Frederick to pour you another cup of tea, Mr Harridge?

HARRIDGE No, I'm all right now. I'm sorry you had to carry me upstairs like that. I don't eat enough, you know, and then when you . . . what was I saying?

MORRISARDE You were asking how I found you. I asked myself what sort of man would have the leisure on a working day to be strolling by the river at mid-morning. Vain enough to carry a walking cane when he could run with his knees raised very high. So frustrated he knocks the heads off flowers. It had to be an unemployed actor. I traced you through a theatrical agency.

HARRIDGE They won't even use me for telly commercials any more. They say my face is worn out. If word spreads I've been talking to moles they'll say my mind's worn out too.

MORRISARDE You mean. . . you won't come to the authorities and corroborate the boy's story?

HARRIDGE It would be curtains for my career.

MORRISARDE It could be curtains for the human race.

HARRIDGE Look. It's not even as if the story were true. All right, I spoke to a mole. You've convinced me. But I don't believe in this great lurking beast, this Magma. I think the moles are pulling our legs.

MORRISARDE But Magma is the Magmazone.

HARRIDGE Magmazone?

MORRISARDE You know that the earth has an outer shell twenty to thirty miles thick? Well, under that there lies an inner layer made of boiling, heaving rock that bubbles like porridge in a saucepan. Now and then, here and there, it bursts up to create an earthquake or a volcanic eruption.

HARRIDGE The Magmazone?

MORRISARDE What the moles were trying to say was that the Magmazone has been so stirred up by man's meddling that it's about to boil out of control and blow the crust to Kingdom Come.

HARRIDGE But d'you seriously believe—d'you seriously maintain it can be stopped by people leaping in the air while the moles of the world unite as a kind of glorified navvy gang?

MORRISARDE It sounds insane, I know. But it's our only hope. Mankind has found no cure for earthquakes. We must pray that molekind has. *Pause.*

HARRIDGE (*in growing excitement*) Mr Morrisarde. Frederick. If an old trouper can help to extend the run of the human follies—on with the motley! (*pause*) And you know, any publicity is good publicity. I shall wear my opera cloak and hat. Where exactly are we going?

MORRISARDE First, to see the Minister for the Environment. *A solo cornet plays a ministerial flourish.*

MORRISARDE It's very kind of you to see us at such short notice, Sir Peter.

SIR PETER Welcome! Welcome, Professor Morrisarde!

FREDERICK (*to himself*) Professor?

SIR PETER When I heard it was you I dropped everything. Won't you and your two, er, colleagues sit down? There. I esteem your visit a great honour, Morrisarde.

MORRISARDE Sir Peter, I have the most urgent message to convey. . . .

SIR PETER (*interrupting*) I have always thought it a tragedy that one of our most original minds should be buried among those Godforsaken moors. London mourns you.

MORRISARDE Sir Peter!

SIR PETER Science mourns you. Knowledge mourns you.

FREDERICK (*whispering*) Mr Harridge—what's that little white button for? In the carpet by his foot?

HARRIDGE (*whispering*) A bell. Shh.

SIR PETER Let me see now. You presented a paper to the Royal Society, as I recall. You'd done some sums suggesting that civilisation would be destroyed by 1990. Some cuffuffle in the Magmazone, wasn't it? You went off in a pet when you were laughed at. Even the Nobel Prize could not console you. And ever since we have lacked. . . .

MORRISARDE (*interrupting*) Sir Peter!

SIR PETER As I was saying, I am continually being bombarded with the most outrageous theories. I had a man in here only the other day who claimed the moon was nothing but an enormous potato. He said the Russians were planning to boil it in the Caspian Sea.

MORRISARDE Sir Peter! Civilisation will be destroyed this year.

SIR PETER This year? Oh, quite, quite.

MORRISARDE And London will be destroyed this Friday unless everybody jumps in the air.

FREDERICK (*whispering*) Sir Peter's just pressed on his bell.

SIR PETER Well, that really is exceptionally interesting, Professor.

The door opens. We hear heavy footsteps.

MORRISARDE Who are these three men?

SIR PETER (*smoothly*) Ah, Hoskins. Professor Morrisarde and his, um, friends are just leaving. It's been absolutely first class, Professor, but I have this meeting on tree preservation this afternoon.

MORRISARDE (*interrupting angrily*) There'll be no trees to preserve if you don't. . . (*he grunts as he is grabbed*).

Hoskins and Co. start ejecting them.

HOSKINS Out you go, grandfather!

MORRISARDE This is criminal assault!

FREDERICK (*to himself*) Why are they throwing us out? One of 'em's got Mr Harridge by the scruff of his opera cloak. His tall hat's slipped over his eyes.

A scuffle as Harridge is bundled out.

HARRIDGE (*angry*) But I was told by a mole!

A flourish from a solo cornet.

Fade out.

85

A busy street.

Mr Morrisarde hails a taxi.

MORRISARDE (*urgently*) New Printing House Square, driver. The Times newspaper. And quickly!

The taxi drives off.

Fade out.

Back in the farmhouse.

We can hear a television set in the background.

UNCLE Well, this is the night. Us'll soon know the truth.

MORRISARDE The second most infamous Friday in history and shown live on
the television. I wonder...if they'd had television in those
days....

FREDERICK I can't wait to see Mr Harridge on the telly.

AUNT It was pure foolishness, telling that story to the newspapers. It's
made fools of you all, it's done London no good and it's turned
my paradise into a slum.

UNCLE Crowds throngin' the gill all week, gapin' at us.

AUNT Laughin' at us.

MORRISARDE Have you noticed how man's laughter is spelled the same as
manslaughter.

UNCLE Diggin' up the mole runs.

AUNT Frightening the cuckoo into the next county. (*pause*) Frederick,
turn up that sound. It's comin' on.

Crash of TV audience applause.

COMPERE Thank you! Thank you, ladies and gentlemen. Thank you and
welcome. And a special big thank you to our studio audience
tonight for having the exceptional courage

Some audience laughter

to join us here in the centre of a London we are assured—yes,
assured—will be swallowed by an earthquake at nine-thirty—
just thirty minutes from now.

Great audience laughter.

COMPERE And also...medals of valour to our—shall we say intrepid?—
our intrepid panel.

Applause and laughter.

And they're going to question Mr Harold Harridge—the man
who says he got news of our impending doom straight from the
horse's—I mean the mole's mouth! Now we see the remote
farmhouse in the Yorkshire Dales where our story begins.

Laughter. Television chat goes on low behind.

UNCLE Fancy, a hundred pound each they offered you and our Frederick

86

to go on this programme, Professor. I'd have grabbed all I could get like that Harold Harridge.

FREDERICK He's very poor. He needs the publicity.

MORRISARDE There are no pockets in a shroud.

UNCLE William Hill is offering ten-thousand to one it won't happen.

AUNT I hope you haven't been chuckin' your money about.

UNCLE Only a quid.

AUNT Your brains want testing.

UNCLE Hush thee now!

COMPERE Now Antonia, what's your reaction to that?

WOMAN ON TV Anyone who believes that is either a charlatan or a simpleton. Sorry, but there it is. Now could you tell me truthfully, Mr Harridge, if you believe in Father Christmas?

Audience laughter.

HARRIDGE Well, it all depends on whether children are watching this programme.

Sarcastic groans from audience.

AUNT Well there's nowt happenin' there. It's just gab gab gab. I'll go and make some supper. Give us a shout if an earthquake comes on.

The door shuts as she leaves.

MAN ON TV Mr Harridge—if London is going to be destroyed tonight, what are you doing here?

Audience laughter.

HARRIDGE Ah, but I won't be here. That's the point. I'm just about to leave. There's a helicopter waiting for me on the roof. (*pause*) Goodbye, folks! Goodbye, London!

Audience boos and hisses.

The television continues in the background as the door opens and Frederick's aunt enters with the tea on a tray.

AUNT (*approaching*) Tea up, lads and lasses. Take this tray off me, Frederick. Still gabbin' on, are they? Makin' a mountain out of a molehill.

UNCLE Hold your tongue, woman, it's nearly the time.

COMPERE ...And it really says something about British pluck, folks, that none of our audience has left the studio. Despite the dire warnings and dramatic exit of our would-be saviour ten minutes ago.

Audience laughter.

And, now, with the hands of the clock just creeping up to nine thirty. . . .

An earthquake hits the television studio.

AUNT Hey, what's wrong wi' picture?

87

MORRISARDE Spinning like a roulette wheel.

UNCLE What's wrong wi' thc sound?

FREDERICK Spinning round and round and zoomin' in and out.

A high pitched signal from the TV set.

It's gone blank.

MORRISARDE You've just seen London dragged down into the arms of the sleeper.

FREDERICK (*in distress*) Can't we do owt to help 'em?

UNCLE We mun leave the dead to bury their dead and see what can be done to save them 'at's still breathing.

A full brass band playing 'Ilkla Moor' as a funeral march.

Fade out.

A few days later. Mr Morrisarde opens the door into the kitchen.

MORRISARDE Good evening, Mrs Spudkins.

AUNT Why come in, Professor, do. I was just saying, we haven't seen hide nor foot of you since London went missing.

MORRISARDE Good evening, Makepeace.

The door closes.

UNCLE Shuffle up on that sofa, Frederick. Make room for the Professor.

MORRISARDE (*gloomily*) Only three days left. I've been taking a long look at the stars.

UNCLE I always liked the stars in the sky.

MORRISARDE The world is ruled by lunatics.

AUNT Weren't that a lovely speech, though, of the new Prime Minister's? "Before the nations can jump together, they must sit down together."

MORRISARDE That's the trouble. They all refuse. Not one of the rulers will even attend the conference he's called in Leeds.

AUNT I do think it's grand, Leeds, being the capital of Britain—even if it is for only one week.

MORRISARDE There are one hundred and forty two sovereign nations and they all want the conference held on their own soil.

FREDERICK Isn't any other country goin' to jump, then?

MORRISARDE They're frightened of losing face. Some say it's all some devilish imperialist plot. Others say the London earthquake was a pure coincidence and had nothing to do with moles.

One country puts all the blame on heavy structures. They've started knocking down all their skyscrapers and turned back ships bringing iron and lead to their ports. They've even dumped all their grand pianos and garden rollers over the border into the next country and caused a war.

88

One poor little nation says it'll jump if the richer ones supply it with free corn and motor cars and hydrogen bombs. Another country will only jump if its neighbour doesn't because they never do anything in common.

In one country the men say they'll order their women to jump but they won't jump themselves. If necessary the women can jump twice. And there's another country where the white men say they'll jump first and the black men can jump later.

There's a civil war going on in one country and neither side will jump in case the other takes advantage and presses home the attack while all the enemy forces are in mid-air. And a group of young people from all over the world have banded together to say they'll sit down at jumping time to show they've got minds of their own.

The dog barks loudly.

FREDERICK   Shut up, Joy!

AUNT   What's up with her?

FREDERICK   Hey, what's happening to the hearthrug?

AUNT   Hearthrug? Why?

UNCLE   That big bulge!

The dog growls.

FREDERICK   It just popped up. It's moving.

AUNT   Towards the edge of the rug.

FREDERICK   Something coming out from under the fringe. It's a—

UNCLE   It's a big white mole!

MORRISARDE   With grass-green eyes as big as pennies.

GUMBOLT   Good evening.

The dog yelps in fear.

AUNT   A talking mole!

GUMBOLT   I am Gumbolt, White Master of Magma. (*pause*) I understand the rulers of the world refuse to attend this conference in Leeds. Tell them *I* will speak. Curiosity might be stronger than national pride.

A solo cornet plays a gay flourish.
A background buzz of many people in a large hall.

FREDERICK   (*awestruck*) This place is even bigger than Skipton Corn Exchange. Hey, Professor, what are all them great silver pipes at the back of the stage?

MORRISARDE   It's an organ.

FREDERICK   Organ? Who're all these people?

MORRISARDE   The rulers of the world's sovereign states. Together for the first time in history.

A fanfare of trumpets.

Here comes Gumbolt.

FREDERICK Carried on a black velvet cushion. (*pause*) They're putting him on that big brass biblestand.

MORRISARDE Hush!

The background buzz ceases. Silence.

GUMBOLT My dear Mankind. If you do not jump it is no great loss. The universe at large will not even notice that another planet is suddenly empty. You will all be dead soon anyway. If the earth rolls on your sons and your grandsons' sons will live. Perhaps that is your wish. It is my wish that my grandsons' sons will live. That is why I am here. We moles have no love for mankind. You have used my people as waistcoats and gloves and as charms against warts and rheumatism. But I suppose you have behaved as badly to one another.

BLUE-SUITED RULER (*yelling from the audience*) Never!

GUMBOLT Would the ruler in the suit of electric blue let me proceed? We moles have cared for the world. You have done your best to harm it. It is wars that have created the weapons so terrible that your rule is drawing to a close. I have been told that man's warring instinct will never die, except with him. It is not true. The Eskimoes and the Congo pygmies have no warfare traditions at all. You have it in you to change your ways. Guard the earth as you guard your money. It is like a fragile egg you must wrap in cotton wool. You must trust your hearts. You must trust one another. You must trust the moles. You rulers of the upper world are frightened that if once your people follow their hearts and act in accord they will want to do it again and again. It is true. And they must.

FUR-HATTED RULER (*yelling from audience*) Never!

GUMBOLT If the ruler in the fur hat will allow me to finish. It will be necessary for all the people on earth to jump every year on June the tenth. For one moment in every year the whole of humanity must be of one mind. In time, they will be of one mind for ever.

BLUE-SUITED RULER Hogwash!

FUR-HATTED RULER Rubbish!

BLUE SUITED RULER It isn't the moles that prop up the earth's crust!

FUR-HATTED RULER It's gravity!

A hum of excited talk throughout the hall.

FREDERICK	Who are those two men? The one in the blue suit and the one in the fur hat?
MORRISARDE	The rulers of the earth's two most powerful nations. This is the first time they've ever agreed about anything. Shhh. *Silence.*
BLUE-SUITED RULER	(*yelling*) You! Mole! It's a game of poker!
FUR-HATTED RULER	(*yelling*) And we're calling your bluff, Gumbolt!
GUMBOLT	(*after a pause*) Very well, we will play poker. But let us play in a meadow. *A solo cornet plays fatefully, as for a battle.*

Fade in murmuring of many people in the open air.

GUMBOLT	Very well, gentlemen. This field will do very nicely. Now if all the rulers except the one in the fur hat and the one in the suit of electric blue will move right back to that blackthorn hedge. Right back, please, your excellencies. *Muttering of retreating rulers.* (*going*) Now, you two come over here. *The two rulers approach.* (*close*) That will do, gentlemen.
BLUE-SUITED RULER	What happens now, Gumbolt?
GUMBOLT	I am going to order the moles who support this portion of the earth's crust to stop working. If nothing happens your excellencies will have won a game of poker.
BLUE-SUITED RULER	How do you mean?
FUR-HATTED RULER	What could happen?
GUMBOLT	A small earthquake of your very own.
BLUE-SUITED RULER	Say, Fur Hat.
FUR-HATTED RULER	Yes?
BLUE-SUITED RULER	We're not going to let an old mole blackmail *us* into capitulation.
FUR-HATTED RULER	He's a classic example of Napoleonic self-aggrandisement.
BLUE-SUITED RULER	We can teach him a thing or two about brinkmanship.
FUR-HATTED RULER	Eyeball to eyeball confrontation. *Pause.*
GUMBOLT	Well, gentlemen?
BLUE-SUITED RULER	Just a minute, for haven's sake! (*pause*) Say, Fur Hat. What say we just get into a huddle over by the hedge? Talk things over?
FUR-HATTED RULER	Talk about talks.
BLUE-SUITED RULER	Sure!
FUR-HATTED RULER	Very well. (*pause*) After you.

91

BLUE-SUITED RULER What d'you mean?

FUR-HATTED RULER You walk to the hedge first, Electric Blue.

BLUE-SUITED RULER Oh, now come on!

FUR-HATTED RULER You walk to the hedge first, then I'll follow.

BLUE-SUITED RULER But if I step down first. . . .

FUR-HATTED RULER It was your idea.

BLUE-SUITED RULER But I want peace with honour. If I step down first it'll be misunderstood. I've got an election coming up.

FUR-HATTED RULER I won't budge unless you budge first.

BLUE-SUITED RULER (*getting ratty*) I could bomb you into budging.

FUR-HATTED RULER (*furiously*) And I'd retaliate a hundredfold.

BLUE-SUITED RULER (*shouting*) Step down—you ignorant bandit!

FUR-HATTED RULER (*shouting*) Unprincipled gangster!

Pause.

GUMBOLT (*very politely*) Well, your excellencies?

Pause.

BLUE-SUITED RULER (*snarling in unison*) We call you, Gumbolt!
FUR-HATTED RULER

The earth creaks and opens. The cries of the two rulers die away as they fall into an abyss.
A solo cornet plays a gay flourish.

Fade in. Open air with cuckoo and bees.

MORRISARDE Well, Frederick. So you climbed up the scar of your own free will. I thought you suffered from vertigo.

FREDERICK I don't get it any more. It's gone like that. And I thought I'd come up here to jump with you. Up on top of the world.

MORRISARDE Looking down on all the earth spread out like a counterpane.

FREDERICK With him underneath, ready to jump out of bed. (*pause*) How long now before we have to jump?

MORRISARDE Only a few minutes. You'll see the Very light shoot up from the church tower. When you see that—jump.

FREDERICK D'you think they'll all jump? Everybody in the world has got to jump if it's to work.

MORRISARDE I've a feeling they will. Mankind's not as mad as it often seems. Maddening perhaps, but not mad. Right up to yesterday the world denied it was going to jump. But all the time every country was secretly making the most elaborate preparations. And they extended to every creature, you know. Animals have been rounded up in the jungles and the deserts and the mountains and herded

92

aboard ships together with the stock of farms and zoos and even circuses. There was no time to train them to jump, but the buoyancy of the water will minimise their weight sufficiently, the scientists believe.

MORRISARDE   The seas today are filled with a million arks. From the mightiest aircraft carrier low in the water with its cargo of hippos and elephants to the leakiest coracle and its crew of pretty bewildered piglets. And ancient flying machines have been wheeled from museums and made ready for the showcase of the clouds. Balloons, Zeppelins, autogyros, helicopters, flying bicycles, flying bedsteads, fighters, bombers, passenger liners—they're all going aloft carrying the animals left over from the ocean fleet.
Pause.

FREDERICK   And to think of folk jumpin' in the jungle! In India and Paris and Stoke-on-Trent. At the same second we jump.

MORRISARDE   (*with a slight chuckle*) And the different nations are going to jump in their own individual ways. One very pious country's going to fill its churches and jump with a prayer. A highly-regimented one will march to sports stadiums and jump saluting the flag. A few lighthearted ones have organised games of jumping over streams or fences or string.
The brass band strikes up 'Ilkla Moor' in the distant village.

FREDERICK   Hark at the brass band in the village. Uncle Makepeace's euphonium's going strong. They're having dancing round the maypole and everything. Makin' a proper feast day of it. And the children are going to play ring a ring o' roses back to front.

MORRISARDE   Back to front?

FREDERICK   Aye—"Atishoo-atishoo, we all jump up!" It's a funny hot wind blowing, Professor. And that sky—I've never seen such a shiny blue. An' it looks stretched tight from horizon to horizon as if it was stretched like a drumskin.

MORRISARDE   It's earthquake weather.

FREDERICK   What'll it be like...what'll happen if they don't all jump? I mean, we'll soon know, won't we?

MORRISARDE   The moment we land we'll know whether all mankind's been jumping with us. If they haven't...you'll see those fells take off like migrating dragons. And then we won't know any more.

FREDERICK   Hey, look yonder! Floating over the fells. Look. Another and another.... Riding the skies above the moor. Dozens of 'em.

MORRISARDE   Balloons. And they're all carrying animals in their gondolas.
Distant aeroplanes join the other sounds.

FREDERICK   And look at them aeroplanes! Gliders. . . .

MORRISARDE Hurricanes and Spitfires.

FREDERICK And look! A 707! There's Concorde!

MORRISARDE I think that's a Lancaster bomber!

FREDERICK Hey, watch out for this balloon with the lambs. (*laughs*) Duck, Professor, it'll just miss our heads.

The bleating of lambs as their balloon passes.

MORRISARDE Are you ready, Frederick? Keep your eyes skinned for that Very light. Only three or four seconds to go.

For two or three seconds all is silent but for a faint bird call and a distant drone of planes. Then a sudden terrific rocket whoosh as the Very light goes up.

FREDERICK (*together*) Up we go!
MORRISARDE

Complete silence for three seconds. Then a cuckoo calls. The brass band strikes up in the village.

FREDERICK (*shouting to Heaven*) Everybody jumped!

The brass band plays at full strength.

Fade out.

Take Any Day
Ivor Wilson

The Cast
1st Attendant

2nd Attendant

Ada Gennet

Old Woman

Dr David Smith

Dakers

Chairman

Caroline Smith

Herbert Dyson

Mollie Dyson

Brenda Duncan

Dr Tenniel

Alice

Mr Jackson

Mrs Gorringe

Mr Owens

Mrs Askew

Betty

Mrs Graham

Dorothy Dinely

Miss Ware

Aileen Telford

Barman

Waiter

Mr Stokesley

Mr Brownlow

Mrs Brownlow

Sergeant

Constable Murphy

Take Any Day

Take Any Day is about some of the pressures of modern life as they weigh upon an individual: in this particular case, a family doctor. David Smith is clever and has made his way from a working-class background, through university into a job which he enjoys. His wife, Caroline, who comes from a comfortable middle-class home, doesn't share his passion for the medical profession and, depressed by the realities of a doctor's life in a small, bleak industrial town, withdraws her support just at the moment when the pressures of work are getting too much for him. He finds some consolation in Aileen, a patient, accommodating woman who loves him and tries to make him take life more easily. He also finds consolation in whisky and in a few months the habit grows to alcoholic proportions.

The action of the play is concentrated on one long explosive day. It begins at three in the morning with a nasty case of abortion, on the day that Caroline decides to leave him for good. There is a row with his partner and a hectic morning in the surgery with too many patients to be seen. Lunch with Aileen is followed by a frustrating non-lovemaking session, and an emergency call to a patient who dies on his hands. Tired and under the influence of alcohol, he faces an evening surgery and end of the day visits. One of these is to an "awkward" household where, after a flare-up and exchange of unpleasantness, David forgets himself and strikes the father of his patient. Within a few moments of leaving he is involved in a minor street accident, breathalysed and found guilty of driving carelessly under the influence of alcohol. Apart from the loss of his licence and the fine for assaulting his patient's father, David faces charges of unprofessional conduct and is struck off the medical register.

The story is told within the framework of a tribunal and ends with a short epilogue which suggests the possibility of his reconciliation with Aileen and return to medicine.

The sounds of an industrial town at night. Shunting train. Milk bottles knocked over and cat howling.
An ambulance approaches—rings bell a couple of times—stops.
The doors open and close as the driver and attendant get out and walk to the rear.

1st ATTENDANT Right, Jack. Let's have that stretcher.

2nd ATTENDANT Coming up, mate.

The sound of the door opening and a stretcher being pulled out.

2nd ATTENDANT What is it this time?

1st ATTENDANT God knows. Emergency of some sort.

2nd ATTENDANT Are they always at three in the morning?

1st ATTENDANT Usually—you'll get used to it. Forty-seven isn't it?

2nd ATTENDANT That's right. The one with the light upstairs.

The sound of the ambulance door banging and footsteps on pavement. Fade out.

A girl moaning—then a sudden cry of pain.

ADA God help me. I'm dying I tell you. (*groans*) I'm dying.

OLD WOMAN You'll be all right, love. You' goin' to 'ospital. They'll look after you.

Ada shrieks again.

SMITH No joke is it?

ADA (*groaning*) It bloody isn't!

SMITH I warned you last time, Ada.

ADA Adeline, doctor, if you don't mind.

SMITH Eh?... Oh! (*laughs*) Ada will do fine for me.

ADA Oh God!

OLD WOMAN Ada!

ADA S'all right for you, you old cow! You're not 'aving it.

SMITH Who did it this time, then?

ADA Who did what?

SMITH Don't be stupid—you know what I mean.

ADA Nowt like that, Doctor. 'onest. I fell on the stairs. Ask me Mam.

OLD WOMAN That she did, doctor. She did. Just after supper. Top to bottom.

SMITH Don't lie, Mrs Gennet. It's Ada's third abortion in two years— she's gone too far on this time. (*angry*) You'll kill yourself in the end, you silly girl.

ADA (*groans*) We'll see. It bloody hurts.

SMITH Well don't expect sympathy. You should damn well come and see me at the right time—not get me out in the middle of the night.

ADA (*groans*) God—I'm sorry, doctor.

SMITH All right—I'll see you when it's over.
A door knocker sounds loudly.

OLD WOMAN That'll be 'ambulance men, doctor.

SMITH Bring them up.

OLD WOMAN Right yo' are, doctor.
She shuffles off. Another knock.
All right, all right—I'm coming.

ADA You'll not tell t'police, doctor?

SMITH (*slightly mocking*) That I will.

ADA Not this time. Please! Oh God it 'urts.
She begins to cry.

ATTENDANT (*approaching*) Here we are again. Doctor Smith?

SMITH That's right.
Ada groans.

ATTENDANT Sounds bad.

SMITH She is.

ATTENDANT Best be moving, then. Come on, Jack, swing your end round. . . .
That's it. Up to the bed. Hard as you can.
Ada is crying softly.
Come on, love—soon have you tucked up safe and sound.
Ada groans.

SMITH Here. Hold it a minute. . . . Steady now—together—Now! That's
it—gently—gently does it. . . . Good. . . . All right, Ada?

ADA (*faintly*) Yes, thanks, doctor.

ATTENDANT Let me pull the blanket up. It's cold outside.

ATTENDANT Right. . . . Watch for the bend on the stairs, Jack.

ADA (*to Smith*) I'll be all right—won't I?

SMITH (*weary*) You'll be in good hands, Ada.

ADA Adeline!

SMITH Adeline, then! You'll be all right.

ADA Thanks, doctor. You're all right yourself.
We hear the attendants struggling downstairs.

WOMAN She *is* all right, doctor, isn't she? I mean, she's not goin' to die,
is she?

SMITH She might. . . . She very easily might. She's lost a lot of blood and
there's bound to be infection.
Woman begins to cry.

SMITH And next time she will die. . . . Remember that when the police
come won't you?
Fade out.

A tribunal in progress.

DAKERS I'm sorry to be so insistent, Sir Joseph, but I feel it is important to establish all the facts about this particular day.

CHAIRMAN The Committee is grateful, Mr Dakers. Your point is that Dr Smith has a difficult practice?

DAKERS Very bad, Sir Joseph.

CHAIRMAN I thought so—but this has never been questioned, Mr Dakers. Dr Smith's practice is typical of many in our oldest industrial cities. They bear the burden of the endemic effect of bad environment—chronic bronchitis, dermatitis, the last pockets of tuberculosis, venereal disease, overloads of births—and deaths. Influenza, warts, and unwanted babies... You would agree?

DAKERS Certainly—but despite this Dr Smith is regarded as an excellent doctor by his colleagues.

CHAIRMAN I agree—and well qualified I see... very well qualified.

DAKERS Most conscientious, Sir Joseph. Never willing to stop until all his patients have been seen.

CHAIRMAN So I understand from his local medical executive. None of this is in dispute, Mr Dakers.

DAKERS My real point is that the day in question began very early for Dr Smith—before three o'clock in the morning to be precise. His wife confirms that it was four before he got home.
Fade out.

The sound of a lavatory flushing and coins being dropped on a hard floor. A chair is knocked over.

SMITH Damn and blast!
Caroline stirs in bed and switches on the light.

CAROLINE Must you make that row.

SMITH Sorry. Sorry. Sorry. I was creeping around in the dark. Thought you were asleep.

CAROLINE Late, aren't you?

SMITH Ada Gennet aborting at five months. Hell of a job.

CAROLINE My God! I bet it was. How many does that make?

SMITH Three.

CAROLINE How?

SMITH Mechanical dilation. Some dirty old cow round the corner I expect.

CAROLINE Bad?

SMITH Fifty-fifty. Bleeding like hell and bound to be infected.
He pours himself a whisky.
(*swallowing*) I needed that. Want one?

CAROLINE At this hour?

SMITH Nobody called?

CAROLINE One. Brownlow, Darley Crescent.

SMITH About the boy David?

CAROLINE Yes.

SMITH Mumps. I was round yesterday morning.

CAROLINE Oh! He sounded pretty agitated.

SMITH Old Father Brownlow would. Bloody snob, and a trouble maker to boot.

CAROLINE He said the boy had a high temperature and you should have called last night.

SMITH And a pig's arse to him.
He pours another whisky.

CAROLINE What did you prescribe?

SMITH Aspirin and bed.

CAROLINE Very good, doctor. . . . I shall miss you.
He gets into bed.

SMITH God this kip's cold. . . . Are you still going?

CAROLINE Yes.

SMITH Pity. You know you don't have to go.

CAROLINE Don't start the row again. Of course I have to. I should have gone two years ago.

SMITH (*bitterly*) I hope it keeps fine for you!
Fade.

The tribunal in progress.

DAKERS Difficult day from the beginning.

CHAIRMAN You mean Dr Smith had been disturbed twice in the night. . . . Did the girl die? The one who aborted?

DAKERS I believe not.

CHAIRMAN Good. So Dr Smith was tired before his day began. Perhaps Mrs Smith can help us here.

CAROLINE Oh yes. Very tired. I remember David fell asleep in the middle of our conversation.

CHAIRMAN And this was not unusual.

CAROLINE Not at all. He was on call at least four nights a week and I've known him get half a dozen telephone calls and have to attend several patients after midnight.

CHAIRMAN But not too often, surely.

CAROLINE Often enough to fall asleep at the drop of a hat—and he *would* get up before six in the morning.

CHAIRMAN Six?

CAROLINE Yes.

CHAIRMAN Good heavens. Was there any specific reason for the early rising Mrs Smith?

CAROLINE He visited patients.

CHAIRMAN At that hour?

CAROLINE David's visiting hours were somewhat elastic, Sir Joseph.

CHAIRMAN So it seems. And he got up early on this particular day?

CAROLINE Yes.

CHAIRMAN Although he had symptoms of an illness which may well have been influenza?

CAROLINE Yes, Sir Joseph.

CHAIRMAN And was dosing himself?

CAROLINE Heavily—I heard him rummaging through the cabinet for aspirin—and he swore because the bottle was empty.

CHAIRMAN The aspirin bottle?

CAROLINE No—he wanted something to drink—to get the aspirin down. What about breakfast?

CAROLINE Hardly any. Some toast I think and coffee.

CHAIRMAN Unwise. Very unwise. And was this common, Mrs Smith?

CAROLINE Most days, Sir Joseph.

CHAIRMAN You didn't get up with him?

CAROLINE No.

CHAIRMAN Oh.

CAROLINE He wouldn't have eaten breakfast if I'd cooked it. We didn't get on—at all.

CHAIRMAN I see.

CAROLINE Once he threw it at me. Bacon, eggs, toast and marmalade. The lot. Just once.

CHAIRMAN Very unfortunate.

CAROLINE Very. I didn't give him an opportunity to repeat the joke.

CHAIRMAN No.—So he departed.

CAROLINE Yes. He took the one 'phone call from Mr Brownlow—it seemed to be unpleasant—and he came upstairs to say goodbye.

CHAIRMAN Quite normal then?

CAROLINE Perfectly—he called me a selfish bitch.

CHAIRMAN Oh!

CAROLINE And I told him to get lost.

     Fade.

DYSON (*after a bit of coughing*) Sorry, doctor.

SMITH Not to worry, Herbert. Take your time.

     Dyson wheezes and splutters.

DYSON Right bad in the morning, it is.

MOLLIE Bad all the time these days an' you know it, Herbert.

SMITH Is it now?

DYSON Niver. Hold your noise, woman.

MOLLIE Flat on the floor with it, coughing his insides out, he is sometimes, not able to get his breath even.

SMITH And he tells me he's improving.

DYSON So I am. Last lot o' tablets made all the difference.

SMITH Glad to hear it. Here let's listen to that chest. Lift your shirt—that's it—stand still—round a bit—breathe in—out—in again. (*pause*) Yes, you're a bit clearer—tuck your shirt in again. I see Rovers won on Saturday.

DYSON Ay. They were lucky mind you. They need a new pack an' Stobbart's not a bit o' bloody use at stand off.

SMITH He can run they tell me.

DYSON Ay, as far as 'lav at half time—an' he should stop there.

MOLLIE Herbert!

SMITH (*laughs*) You were there, then?

DYSON Ay. It were a bit on the damp side I admit.

SMITH It were!

DYSON Ah wrapped up well though.

MOLLIE I saw to that, doctor—two pullovers and a scarf.

SMITH Still smoking too, Herbert.

DYSON Ay! An odd tab now and again like.

SMITH Make sure that's all it is Herbert. You're chronic—and bronchitis kills. I've explained what it does to your lungs and heart often enough.

DYSON You 'ave, doctor—but ah'm sixty-eight and at my age ah reckons ah'm entitled to some'at else beyond 'pension—if it's on'y a few tabs and bronchitis. (*pause*) Time to finish our game o' chess before you go?

SMITH Make it tomorrow, Herbert. I want to see Brenda's baby before surgery—and it could be a busy day.

DYSON Right you are, doctor. . . . Don't overdo it now.

SMITH I won't.

Fade.

The tribunal.

CHAIRMAN But of course that's exactly what Dr Smith did?

DAKERS Yes, Sir Joseph.

With at least one more visit before surgery. . . . Brenda wasn't it? Brenda Duncan. Unmarried mother with three children. Lives

in a sordid second storey room in a very poor slum.
Fade.

Smith bangs on the door and opens it.

SMITH 'Morning, Brenda.

BRENDA Hello, doctor—you are early. Just feeding baby.

SMITH Go on—don't stop. Got enough milk have you?

BRENDA Plenty, doctor.

SMITH That's something—thought I'd catch you before surgery—How is she?

BRENDA Lovely, doctor.

SMITH Been sick again?

BRENDA No, doctor.

SMITH She looks all right. But she's not out of the wood yet.

BRENDA I know, doctor.

SMITH Keep her warm and don't let the others feed her scraps.

BRENDA I won't.

SMITH Not even Grandma.

BRENDA I won't, doctor—Really.

SMITH How's Jimmy's leg?

BRENDA Cleared up doctor. (*sniffing*) We've all got colds, doctor.

SMITH I'm not surprised—in this damned hole. (*pause*) Here's a prescription—something for your colds. Brown for you. Red for the kids. Don't pour it down the sink.

BRENDA Thanks, doctor. I won't. Like a cup of tea?

SMITH Thank you, Brenda, no—How's that cut on your head? Look at the window—not bad—not bad. You're lucky.

BRENDA Yes doctor.

SMITH And the ribs?

BRENDA All right.

SMITH And if I press a little.

BRENDA Ow!

SMITH Fine. Just like a heavyweight—after the fight. You're well rid of that boyo—He really marked you.

BRENDA I know. But he was such a lovely fella. Scotch you know. Never a bad word out of him. All lovey dovey. Telly on H.P. New coat. Took me out to 'club every Tuesday. Then he got in with some fellas off a ship. Came back drunk and gave me a good hiding. Took all my Social Security too, doctor; every penny. . . . An' look at my puddings.

SMITH Your what?

BRENDA Christmas puddings. He fancied 'em so I made six. Look—

She opens the cupboard.

A cupboardful of bloody puddings.

SMITH *(laughs)* You never learn do you, Brenda. You pick up dead beats like stray cats and all you get out of them is a good hiding and another baby.

BRENDA I know, doctor. I'm soft with 'em. I can't 'elp it.

SMITH Not this time I hope, Brenda? Not another one for God's sake!

BRENDA Yes, doctor. I've missed two.

SMITH You can't go on like this. The Council'll take the children into care.

BRENDA They won't!

SMITH They will that. What've you got the bucket of water for? Another leak?

BRENDA No. Bloody landlord's turned the water off up here till we pay extra rent. I bring it up from the yard in a bucket.

SMITH You carry it up yourself, up those stairs?

BRENDA Three a day.

SMITH You'll kill yourself.... I'll chase up the Health Department about it...and get off to the clinic yourself and let the nurse keep an eye on you.
Fade.

The tribunal.

CHAIRMAN Unorthodox.

DAKERS Yes.

CHAIRMAN Interfered with things not really in his province.

DAKERS Well, Sir Joseph—

CHAIRMAN Come, Mr Dakers. Here's the letter he sent to the Medical Officer. Pretty strong. . . . And what about the one he sent to the Council for Unmarried Mothers. Wrote to them saying mothers were mothers. Having a gold ring on the finger didn't sanctify the process. He advised the council to stop behaving like a set of charitable virgins or join a nunnery. Hardly diplomatic was it?

DAKERS Rather blunt, I admit, Sir Joseph. One of his patients needed special financial assistance and couldn't get any.

CHAIRMAN Really? And what about the thirty odd letters to the Local Council about accommodation schemes?

DAKERS Impulsive, perhaps.

CHAIRMAN Perhaps! And so apparently were some of his other communications—to the Ministry of Health, the Regional Hospital Board, the local Health Executive, his MP, the Welfare Services Officer and so on and so on. It can't have made him popular?

DAKERS No, Sir Joseph. He tended to write in the heat of the moment.

CHAIRMAN But not to regret it!

DAKERS It seems not.

CHAIRMAN And how did all this irregular visiting and letter writing affect his work in the practice? Dr Tenniel, as the senior partner perhaps you can tell us.

TENNIEL On the whole for good, Sir Joseph. No complaints from me. David—Dr Smith did a great deal for the practice. More than his fair share.

CHAIRMAN But occasionally he was unreliable?

TENNIEL *(hesitates)* Well—yes. We had our differences of opinion—mostly about surgery times and punctuality.

CHAIRMAN Including the day in question.

TENNIEL Yes—we had a few words about it.

CHAIRMAN Rather a poor start to the day.

TENNIEL I suppose it was.

CHAIRMAN Not out of the ordinary, then?

TENNIEL Honestly—no. Of course his domestic scene was pressing somewhat, but it had been brewing for months. We were both inclined to be edgy in the morning and David—Dr Smith had this irritating habit of being a few minutes late for surgery.

CHAIRMAN Regularly.

TENNIEL Frequently. Almost a matter of pride with him.
Fade.

A baby crying.

ALICE Morning, Dr Smith.

SMITH Morning, Alice. Busy already?

ALICE Twenty past doctor. Surgery's full.

SMITH It would be—and here's Robert.

TENNIEL *(approaching along the corridor)* David! Where the hell have you been?

SMITH Eh? Visiting a few cronies. Surgery started?

TENNIEL Come off it. You know damn well it's twenty past nine. We have no right to keep these people waiting.

SMITH No. Of course not. Sorry, Robert. Didn't think it was so late.

TENNIEL It's our big day, man. Friday. At the rate they're coming we'll have sixty or seventy and I've got the bloody hospital committee at ten-thirty.
A phone rings in the background. Alice answers it.

SMITH God! So you have. Warm in here, isn't it.

TENNIEL You all right.

SMITH   Head. 'Flu maybe. Don't worry, I'll dose myself up.

ALICE   (*calling along the corridor*) For you, Dr Smith. Dr Batsford in the Infirmary. I said you'd ring back in a few minutes.

SMITH   Thanks, Alice.

TENNEIL   Batsford? What does he want?

SMITH   Ada Gennet aborted. Three this morning. I sent her in to him.

TENNIEL   Didn't know she was pregnant. You left her alone, I hope.

SMITH   Like the plague. One shot in the arm and then telephoned for the bloodwagon. Left the dirty work to Batsford.

TENNIEL   Good. You're learning at last. She should be on the pill— shouldn't she?

SMITH   Won't. Says it makes her sick. . . .

TENNIEL   And me.

SMITH   Brenda's in the club again.

TENNIEL   God! Can't you think of anything good to tell me. . . . By the way Brownlow rang at nine.

SMITH   His boy has mumps.

TENNIEL   I know—but he's persistent.

SMITH   Bloody troublemaker.

TENNIEL   I know—but he has friends on the Council.

SMITH   We should chuck him off our list.

TENNIEL   Now, David. Let's not start that again.

SMITH   All right. All right. We can't afford to lose one. We only have seven thousand on the list.

TENNIEL   It isn't that either.

SMITH   No? Anything important you want me to see today.

TENNIEL   Granny Soames. She'll probably snuff it today. Alice'll remind you. . . . And there's the accountant's report. . . . He can't read your bloody figures. (*he laughs*) Sorry I blew my top. . . . Don't overdo things will you—you look shocking.

SMITH   (*wryly*) I'll try not to. Enjoy your weekend if I don't see you before you go.

TENNIEL   Thanks. . . . (*tentatively*) No developments à la Caroline?

SMITH   No change. Kids have gone to Grandmother. Caroline's following this weekend.

TENNIEL   I'm sorry, David. (*he goes, closing the door behind him*)

SMITH   I know—I wish I was.

    He flicks the switch on the intercom.

ALICE   (*distorted*) Yes, doctor?

SMITH   We're in action, Alice. Get me Batsford on the 'phone.

ALICE   Yes doctor.

    Click as the intercom goes dead.

He pours himself a whisky.
Phone rings.

SMITH Batsford? Yes. Smith here. . . . Yes that's right. Ada Gennet. . . .
I see. Bad as that. . . . I thought it didn't look so good. . . .
Nothing *I* could do at that stage—that's why I bunged her in—
She's as strong as a horse anyhow. I know. . . . Not reported to
us of course. . . . Some old biddy round the corner no doubt. Tell
the sergeant to lean on her old hag of a mother as hard as he
can. . . . OK—thanks for ringing—Bye.

He puts the phone down. Flicks intercom.

ALICE (*distorted*) Yes.

SMITH Wheel 'em in.

ALICE (*distorted*) Mr Jackson, Dr Smith will see you now. Second door
on the left down the corridor.

SMITH Busy?

ALICE (*distorted*) Twenty visits already, doctor—and there's Dr
Tenniel's regulars to see.

SMITH Thanks! —Any news of Mrs Hope?

ALICE (*distorted*) Went in this morning.

SMITH Already?

A knock on the door.

Come in. (*to Alice*) Only needs Mary Jenkins and that little
scrubbing woman to go bang a day early and I'll be labouring
all night again.

The intercom clicks off.

SMITH Now, Mr Jackson. Sit down.

He looks at the patient's file.

Let's see, it's your back, isn't it?

JACKSON You said if it didn't get any better—

SMITH And it isn't?

JACKSON No. Fair kills me.

SMITH Stand up.

JACKSON Eh?

SMITH Stand up, man.

The chair scrapes.

Turn round. I want to find the exact spot.

Jackson groans.

There, is it?

JACKSON All round there.

SMITH All right, sit down. . . . I'm going to send you for an X-ray and
let Mr Bennet at the hospital have a look.

He flicks the intercom.

And the next, Alice.
The intercom clicks off.
Now it may be a day or two. Keep on with the treatment. I'll write you up for some new stuff.... Get these from the chemist. They'll help with the pain.
A knock on the door.

JACKSON   Right, doctor.
Come in! 'Bye Mr Jackson.
The door opens. We hear a baby crying.
Ah. Now what is it, Mrs Gorringe?

MRS GORRINGE   It's the baby again, doctor. 'e cries all the time.

SMITH   Sounds like it. Bring him here where I can see him properly. (*pause*) He's still dirty, Mrs Gorringe! Look at his legs. Scabies! It's a dirt disease.

MRS GORRINGE   'e cries, doctor.

SMITH   Of course he cries! He's dirty and uncomfortable. He wets the bed. He smells of it.

MRS GORRINGE   Yes, doctor.

SMITH   Now take him home and give him a bath.

MRS GORRINGE   'aven't got a bath, doctor.

SMITH   Wash him in a bowl then! And get this from the chemist. Put it on all those patches as quick as you can.

MRS GORRINGE   Yes, doctor.

SMITH   And it wouldn't do any harm to have a good wash yourself—you wouldn't want what he's got, would you?

MRS GORRINGE   No, doctor. (*she goes closing the door behind her*)
Intercom flicks.

ALICE   (*distorted*) Yes, doctor?

SMITH   Next one.

ALICE   (*distorted*) Mr Owens! Second door on the left.

SMITH   The Gorringe baby has scabies after all I've said. Get on to the Welfare people, will you.... Oh and send them round to 41 Spring Street. Brenda Duncan's having trouble with the landlord again—and she's pregnant.
The door opens.
Certificate, is it?

OWENS   (*wheezing*) That's right, doctor.

SMITH   Chest?

OWENS   Dust, doctor.

SMITH   Foundry?

OWENS   S'right, doctor.

SMITH   Getting any better?

OWENS No, doctor.

SMITH Can't have everything, can we. Here you are.

OWENS Thank you, doctor. (*he goes, closing the door behind him*)

The telephone rings.

Dr Smith. Yes, Mrs Ryan. How many times?... Has she a temperature?... Yes keep her in bed. What number is it? Yes. Twenty-five. Got that. Thank you. I'll see you today.

He puts the phone down.

A tap on the door.

Come in.

MRS ASKEW Mrs Askew, doctor.

SMITH Yes?

MRS ASKEW It's Mr Askew, doctor.

SMITH Is it?

MRS ASKEW Yes—you know—the shingles.

SMITH Of course. How is he, Mrs Askew?

MRS ASKEW Like he always is doctor—bad tempered.

SMITH (*laughs*) Shingles are hardly a joke, Mrs Askew. I'll call in and see him in a day or two.

The intercom buzzes.

Here's something to cool him down.

Intercom switch.

Yes, Alice.

MRS ASKEW Thank you, doctor.

ALICE (*distorted*) Dr Tenniel's gone.

SMITH All right, Mrs Askew. (*pause*) (*to Alice*) What was that?

ALICE (*distorted*) Dr Tenniel's just gone. I'll have to switch his patients to you.

SMITH That's what I thought you said. Hold them for five minutes, Alice. I have some paper work to catch up.

ALICE (*distorted*) Would you like some coffee now?

SMITH Coffee? Great! Did you get Mrs Baxter's specimen?...

ALICE (*distorted*) Yes, doctor. And there's three other samples.

SMITH Good! That's right.... Baxter, Jones, Ackroyd—and there'll be X-ray letters for Owen and Mossman....

ALICE (*distorted*) Mrs Smith's been ringing.

SMITH Who? Caroline?... Get her for me, will you—And find some aspirins to go with the coffee.

Intercom clicks.

He pours a whisky.

The telephone rings.

Caroline? Now what is it? The milk? What's wrong with the

milk? How many pints will I need? How the hell do I know.... You do that! You do just that! You can do just what the hell you like.... Thank you. Thank you very much.... A postcard will do. One of those with fat ladies prominently displayed! (*suddenly quiet and serious*) I'm sorry! It's a busy surgery and my head's killing me. No. *I think* I understand.... Robert sends you his good wishes.... Said he was sorry.... Yes.... So am I. Thanks for ringing anyway. Civilised to the end. 'Bye.
He puts the phone down.
Fade.

The tribunal.

CHAIRMAN Certainly a pretty hectic day.

DAKERS Fifteen certificates, two examinations, twelve prescriptions, twenty-nine patients altogether before ten-thirty.

CHAIRMAN And twelve to come. And that particular telephone call was hardly likely to improve the situation.
I'm afraid not. But he hardly had time to brood.
Fade.

Smith is washing his hands.

SMITH And you're not pregnant.

BETTY No, doctor.

SMITH Sure?

BETTY Yes, doctor.

SMITH But you had intercourse.

BETTY (*hesitates*) Yes, doctor.

SMITH Regularly?

BETTY (*hesitates*) Yes, doctor. But Ronnie went to Spain for his holiday. He said he had an injection. That made him safe for three months.

SMITH Ronnie's safe enough. It's you I'm worried about. How many have you missed?

BETTY Two, doctor.

SMITH And been sick.

BETTY Yes, doctor.

SMITH I think we'd best have a test—just to make sure—don't you, Betty?

BETTY Yes, doctor.... Mi' mam'll kill me when she finds out.
A knock on the door.

SMITH Come in, Mrs Graham!
The door opens.
(*to Betty*) Specimen in for today's laboratory parcel and I'll be

able to tell you on Monday—and don't worry till then.

BETTY No, doctor. (*she goes*)

SMITH Now, Mrs Graham. How's the head?

MRS GRAHAM Not much better, doctor.

SMITH Sit in the chair and I'll have another look at your eyes.
She sits down.
That's right.... Look up.... Down.... Left.... (*pause*) Nothing obvious but we'll make sure. Can't live for ever on tea and aspirin. Eyes first. Appointment with Mr Nolan.
The intercom buzzes.
You'll get a card. Three or four weeks I should think.

MRS GRAHAM Thank you, doctor.

SMITH All right, Mrs Graham.
The intercom clicks.
Yes?

ALICE (*distorted*) Miss Telford ringing you, doctor.

SMITH Who? Oh, Aileen.... Put her through.
Intercom clicks off. He picks up the telephone.
Hello, Aileen.

MRS GRAHAM Goodbye, doctor.

SMITH Hold on a minute.... 'Morning, Mrs Graham. We'll get in touch as soon as the result comes in.... (*pause*) (*into phone*) No, it's fine—just in the middle of surgery. No.... Robert's off to one of his bloody medical meetings....
The door closes as Mrs Graham goes.

SMITH Still a dozen or so to get through before visits.... The usual coughs and colds and bad backs, couple of teenage mums-to-be and a collier who wanted to slug me because I wouldn't fill in his certificate and post-date it.... Medicine at its best, I'd say.
He pours another whisky.
Caroline? Gone.... Permanently.... Yeh.... It'll make a difference.... I'll miss the kids.... A difference to us?... Well, of course it's a good thing.... Let me get over the shock.
A knock on the door.
Look I've a patient at the door. I'll ring you.... Lunch? (*reflects*) Yes. I suppose I'll have to get used to the idea.... Okay, I'll see you at the Beech Tree, one sharp...'bye.
He puts the phone down.
Come in!
Door opens.
Oh, it's you, Alice—All done then?

ALICE All but one, doctor.

SMITH   Not a bad second half. Two painful periods. One tonsils, three chest, one hypochondriac, one certifiable insane, two varicose ulcers and a trapped finger.... Did you get the specimens?

ALICE   Yes, doctor.

SMITH   Sorry. I remember—I asked earlier. I suppose the last one's Mrs Dinely?

ALICE   Yes—she's outside.... Can I take the medical records?

SMITH   All yours—
A gentle tap on the door.
Come in, Dorothy.... Come for your heart-to-heart I expect.

DOROTHY   Yes, David.

SMITH   Come and sit down then. I like my patients to be in striking distance.
He pours two drinks.
Here let's be sociable.

DOROTHY   It's that bad?

SMITH   Just a quick snort among friends.

DOROTHY   You shouldn't.

SMITH   Don't worry. I'm celebrating my last patient of the morning! *(laughs)* I have lunch before the real business of the day starts.

DOROTHY   What about it?
He consults her file.
I have to know, David. If it's really bad I have to make arrangements for the kids and the shop. Richard can't cope with it all.

SMITH   It's not good.

DOROTHY   It's what we thought.

SMITH   Blood counts, stains, the lot. Lymphocytic leukemia—in a very early stage.

DOROTHY   Thanks. At least we know.

SMITH   It could be worse.

DOROTHY   Oh? How long have I got, six months?

SMITH   Don't be in such a damned hurry to get away from us.

DOROTHY   Longer?

SMITH   Remember the night of Ratty's party?

DOROTHY   When you first told me you fancied me?

SMITH   Was it? *(laughs)* Well?

DOROTHY   December 23rd, 1964—just after one, half-way up the stairs. I said I fancied you too.

SMITH   You surprise me.

DOROTHY   I do? Then how about what happened on the evenings of the 28th and 29th.

SMITH   Amnesia—that was before our relationship became professional.

DOROTHY More's the pity—well what about 1964?

SMITH If they'd diagnosed leukemia then I'd have said two years for you at the most.

DOROTHY And now?

SMITH Five with luck. Much better chemotherapy, new compounds and better use of old ones. If they go on improving at the present rate it could be considerably longer.

DOROTHY (*relieved*) That's not bad is it?

SMITH That's damned good, Mrs Dorothy Dinely. Suspended sentence —and maybe a free pardon.

DOROTHY I'll take it—gladly.

SMITH Thanks—I didn't want to tell you.

DOROTHY I know—but I'd have made you.

SMITH How about Richard?

DOROTHY In good time. I'll just go on being anaemic. (*hesitantly*) What about the other?

SMITH What other?

DOROTHY The specialist talked about removing....

SMITH Oh, a breast. Just rumour I assure you.... You vain old thing.... Not even considered.

DOROTHY Thank God for that! I dreaded that part of it.
She kisses him.

SMITH Hey, steady. What about my reputation.

DOROTHY (*she laughs—then is suddenly serious*) Has Caroline gone?

SMITH Today.

DOROTHY Oh, David! How terrible.

SMITH Yes. It's funny. There she was this morning. Like every other morning. Grumpy when I got in early. Asleep when I left. I forgot to ask her about clean socks. Nine years is a long time.

DOROTHY But it was really finished years ago.

SMITH Four or five.

DOROTHY You shouldn't have stuck it.

SMITH Can't blame Caroline. It was pretty lousy for her too. We just stopped hitting it off—and started hitting each other instead. Anyway, it's over.

DOROTHY You can't look after the house and yourself.

SMITH Not looking forward to it, certainly.
Any plans?

SMITH Not in that direction.... Just as far as lunch today.
Fade.

The tribunal.

CHAIRMAN A convenient time to take stock I think, Mr Dakers. Nothing extraordinary so far.

DAKERS No. Of course he had been seeing patients pretty well non-stop for two hours.

CHAIRMAN Ordinary enough these days I fancy, Dr Tenniel.

TENNIEL In our practice certainly.

CHAIRMAN How long since Dr Smith joined you?

TENNIEL Five years, one as assistant, four as partner.

CHAIRMAN And before that?

TENNIEL Three assistants. One of them lasted eight months. They came after Dr Rogers died. He had a heart attack.

CHAIRMAN And how old was Dr Rogers?

TENNIEL Fifty-four when he died.

CHAIRMAN Fifty-four. (*pause*) Why is the practice hard?

TENNIEL Overloaded with chronics, the old and heavy industrials. Too many children and too many certificates to sign.

CHAIRMAN But you've lasted, Dr Tenniel. You don't look worn out or depressed, if you don't mind me saying so.

TENNIEL I haven't Dr Smith's temperament.

CHAIRMAN Perhaps you'd explain.

TENNIEL It worried him that behind the daily traffic of trivial ailments and form-filling he was missing the really sick.

CHAIRMAN Which might explain his eccentricity over visits?

TENNIEL It might.

CHAIRMAN Mr Dyson? Dr Smith called on you at some odd times, didn't he?

DYSON Any time after five in the morning. (*he coughs*) Can do nowt for your chest, 'erbert, he'd say, except 'old it at bay, but ah'll give thee a beating at chess.

CHAIRMAN And did he?

DYSON (*chuckles*) Not always. (*coughs*) Knew what 'e wor doin' though, mek no mistake. Did me a damn sight better than the pills I'm tekkin' I'll tell thee.

CHAIRMAN (*laughs*) Glad to hear it Mr Dyson. And what about Mrs Dinely— would you agree with Mr Dyson's appreciation of Dr Smith's talent?

DOROTHY Yes.

CHAIRMAN But yours must have been a very painful interview, Mrs Dinely.

DOROTHY Not in the least, Sir Joseph. When I went in of course I was afraid and depressed but somehow David made it seem so hopeful. I felt almost elated when I left.

CHAIRMAN You surprise me.

DOROTHY I was happier than I'd been for years. I still am, Sir Joseph. Five years and a little hope. It's—it's wonderful.

CHAIRMAN You are close friends?

DOROTHY Very close.

CHAIRMAN And no more? I am sorry to have to ask.

DOROTHY I'm very fond of David.

CHAIRMAN You are?

DOROTHY Yes—but so are lots of others. He's that kind of man.

CHAIRMAN I think I'm beginning to understand that.

DOROTHY We became friends three years ago.... We might have become more but he insisted I became a patient to stop it. I'm really on Dr Tenniel's list but David—Dr Smith—looks after me and my family.

CHAIRMAN As a doctor?

DOROTHY Yes.

CHAIRMAN And nothing more?

DOROTHY And nothing more. Absolutely not.

DAKERS I would have thought, Sir Joseph, there was no suggestion of Dr Smith being involved in this way.

CHAIRMAN No serious suggestion, Mr Dakers, but if I understand aright, on the day Dr Smith's wife left him he had lunch with another woman—a Miss Telford?

DAKERS Yes. There was the telephone call. Miss Telford was a friend.

MISS WARE Too friendly if you ask me.

CHAIRMAN Name please.

MISS WARE Mavis Ware.

CHAIRMAN Dr Smith saw you that morning?

MISS WARE That's my business.

CHAIRMAN I see.

MISS WARE He was no gentleman.

CHAIRMAN Oh! Why not?

MISS WARE His accent. And he once used the word—arse.

CHAIRMAN He did?

MISS WARE Said Mr Atkins didn't know his—arse—from his elbow.

CHAIRMAN Mr Atkins?

MISS WARE My chiropodist.

CHAIRMAN But you were quite happy with Dr Smith's medical skill?

MISS WARE Oh he was a good enough doctor—but that's not what we're talking about—are we?

CHAIRMAN Aren't we? It was apparently not the first time Dr Smith and Miss Telford had met alone socially.

DAKERS No.

CHAIRMAN Miss Telford?

AILEEN Regularly, Sir Joseph.

CHAIRMAN How long? Weeks? A few months?

AILEEN Almost two years, Sir Joseph.

CHAIRMAN Although Dr Smith was married?

AILEEN Although he was married.

CHAIRMAN And Mrs Smith approved?

CAROLINE I was quite indifferent, Sir Joseph.

CHAIRMAN I see, Mrs Smith.... You surprise me a little.... Even when you first became aware of it?

CAROLINE I introduced him to Aileen.... We were friends.

CHAIRMAN Friends.... Still?

CAROLINE Not enemies at least, Sir Joseph.... If Aileen wants to take on another problem, she's welcome. I've had enough.

CHAIRMAN The marriage is broken then?

CAROLINE We didn't get on. The last two or three years were misery.

CHAIRMAN How long were you married?

CAROLINE Nine years.

CHAIRMAN Children?

CAROLINE Two. A boy eight, a girl six.

CHAIRMAN And when did it begin to break up?

CAROLINE Five or six years ago.

CHAIRMAN Any apparent reason?

CAROLINE I don't like being a doctor's wife. Not this doctor anyway.

CHAIRMAN I see. And sexual relations? I'm sorry to have to ask about these things.

CAROLINE Stopped about the same time—except when we were tipsy after a party. Not at all for the last couple of years.

CHAIRMAN So he might look elsewhere.

BARMAN Plenty where, if you ask me. Four or five different ones at the Country Club. Sometimes lunch, sometimes dinner. If you ask me....

CHAIRMAN We are not asking you, Mr Alder—You're the barman at the Club?

BARMAN That's right. From where I stand you see plenty. He had the touch all right. Some of them were right young tarts. I wanted to ask him how he did it. I never get that sort holding my hand.

CHAIRMAN Can we concentrate on Miss Telford?

BARMAN The last one? Well she was different. Classy. Quiet but willing I'd say. Real thing. If you asks me they were stuck on each other. Lunch three times a week. Mooning over the brandy.
Fade.

The sounds of a country club dining room. Subdued talk and piped music.

SMITH Shouldn't have come.

AILEEN Sorry!

SMITH Not you. Work's on my mind.

AILEEN Forget it.

SMITH Twenty visits—and evening surgery still to come.

AILEEN Forget it!

SMITH OK. Till two.... But I *have* to go by two, remember—at the very latest.

AILEEN I'll remember.

WAITER You want to order, Sir?

SMITH Same as usual?

AILEEN Fine.

SMITH Fruit juice—Soup—Two mixed grills—One ice cream—Two coffees—Brandy.

WAITER Yes, Sir.

SMITH And a couple more sherries and a bottle of burgundy with the grills.

WAITER Yes, Sir.

AILEEN *(laughs)* You do it in the manner born, Dr Smith.

SMITH *(not laughing)* Honours in nose picking. My Council School background coming out.

AILEEN That's not like you, David.

SMITH Not my day.

AILEEN I thought medicine was a vocation.

SMITH You can have too much of a vocation.

AILEEN You wouldn't do anything else.

SMITH No? I'm beginning to wonder.

Fade.

The tribunal.

BARMAN Just like the other days. Eat, drink, and look miserable. Then off. In that little buggy of his. And it wouldn't need three guesses to say where.

CHAIRMAN We don't know where.

AILEEN My room. We made love.

BARMAN You could tell what they were after.

AILEEN He was married. There wasn't much future in it for me.

CHAIRMAN The possibility of marriage was never mentioned?

AILEEN I loved him. It didn't matter.

CHAIRMAN And on this particular occasion?

AILEEN I nagged him into coming. He wanted to be on his visits by

two. . . . We quarrelled about it. . . . But he came (*laughs*) Not very
exciting really. . . . He fell asleep on me. . . . And that was that.

BARMAN I knew what they were up to. Still it takes all sorts to make a
world I always say. (*laughter*)
Fade.

A bed creaks

SMITH (*waking*) Caroline?

AILEEN Sorry—only me.

SMITH Oh!

AILEEN You fell asleep.

SMITH God. What's the time?

AILEEN Almost two. I was going to wake you.

SMITH Damn. I'm late.

AILEEN I'll make a drink.

SMITH Don't bother. I haven't time. (*The sound of water running in a basin.*)
Sorry, love.

AILEEN Doesn't matter.

SMITH Of course it matters.

AILEEN All right—it does. I shouldn't have tried today.

SMITH No! That's for sure.

AILEEN You'll ring me?

SMITH Yes.

AILEEN When?

SMITH Give me the weekend to sort myself out.

AILEEN Tomorrow.

SMITH All right. If it's that important. Tomorrow.

AILEEN There should be a society.

SMITH There should?

AILEEN For the prevention of sex-starved women. . . . It's funny.

SMITH What is?

AILEEN Now you can have me—on a plate—I don't think you want me
at all.

SMITH You're being silly.

AILEEN Am I?. . . You haven't asked me to marry you yet.

SMITH You know why.

AILEEN No reason at all.

SMITH That's stupid. . . . I have to go.

AILEEN Yes. I know. I'm a selfish bitch.

SMITH 'Bye.

AILEEN 'Bye.

SMITH I'll ring. (*he goes*)

AILEEN Yes. Do that.
Fade.

The tribunal

CHAIRMAN Not a very happy parting, Miss Telford.

AILEEN I'm not complaining.

CHAIRMAN You were used to it perhaps?

AILEEN Being frustrated? With David it's a sort of national pastime. Will he, won't he, can he, can't he.

CHAIRMAN I see.

AILEEN I'm glad. It helps.

CHAIRMAN You agree, Mrs Smith?

CAROLINE More or less. Not that I can claim quite so much experience as Aileen these last few years.

CHAIRMAN But it was one of the reasons for your bad relations with your husband?

CAROLINE Of course. But not a very important one. More a symptom than a reason I'd say.
Fade.

A telephone rings. Alice picks up the receiver.

ALICE Dr Smith? Oh I am glad you called. There's a message from Stokesley, 14 Grey Street.... Yes, Elspeth.... Had an attack.... Pretty bad, I think.... No—less than ten minutes ago.... I've been ringing the club.... Yes.... Right, doctor, I'll hang on in case.
Fade.

A doorbell rings. A door opens.

MR STOKESLEY Thank God you've come, doctor. It's a bad one this time.

SMITH Right, Tom. Don't stop me.
He hurries upstairs. Sound of shallow, noisy breathing.

STOKESLEY It's her colour that's so bad.

SMITH Right. Push the cylinder over.... Get the mask on her face.... That's it.... Just a—quick—injection. Don't look, man.... That's it.... Stay out a minute, Mrs Stokesley.
The breathing becomes quieter.

STOKESLEY Seems better, doctor. She's recognised you.

SMITH Good. There you are my lovely lass. Thought I said you weren't to frighten us again.... Here, Tom, hold this for a minute, while I get my jacket off. (*pause*) Don't let the mask slip now. (*pause*)

STOKESLEY Doctor!

SMITH All right, Tom?

STOKESLEY I don't know, doctor. I think she's stopped.

SMITH Look out—Heart's gone! Give me a bit of room, will you.... Let's see if massage will help.... (*he is breathing heavily*) Get that syringe for me.... That's the one...and the little red box.... Thanks.... We can only try.... We can only try....

STOKESLEY Yes. Please, doctor. Anything. Please—anything, anything, anything.
Fade.

SMITH (*sighs*) I'm sorry, Tom.

STOKESLEY Elspeth?

SMITH She's gone.... For good.

STOKESLEY All over is it?

SMITH Lived on her heart too long. It couldn't take it any longer.

STOKESLEY No.

SMITH Sorry, Tom. Damn sorry. Damn sorry.

STOKESLEY Can't be helped. You did your best. Nobody could a' done more. You warned us how she'd go suddenly. Didn't think it would be today though.

SMITH We never do. I'll give you something for Doris if you like.

STOKESLEY Thanks. She's going to break her heart.
Fade.

The tribunal.

CHAIRMAN And there really was nothing else Dr Smith could have done, Dr Tenniel?

TENNIEL Nothing.

CHAIRMAN But he worried about those few lost minutes he'd spent with Miss Telford?

TENNIEL Yes. He felt bad about that. If he'd stayed on at the Beech Tree Club he'd have got the message a minute or two earlier.

CHAIRMAN It made no difference?

TENNIEL Absolutely none. With the equipment available he did as much or more than any other GP in those circumstances.

CHAIRMAN But if he'd arrived a little earlier there might have been time to get her to hospital where there was more equipment?

TENNIEL No. Perhaps a two hundred mile trip to the Royal Chest Hospital might have prolonged her life for a few hours. No more. The postmortem showed that conclusively. Twenty years of struggling for life had worn out Elspeth's heart. It stopped and all the adrenalin in the world couldn't start it again.

CHAIRMAN And *after* Miss Stokesley died?

TENNIEL Dr Smith got his secretary to contact the hospital to see to the postmortem. He then finished his afternoon visits.

CHAIRMAN Getting home about four thirty.

TENNIEL An empty house—no meal—and another surgery ahead of him—perhaps three hours work.

CHAIRMAN I can see how the pressure was building up. Was it usually such a busy day, Dr Tenniel?

TENNIEL Yes. But normally we would have shared it. The practice is arranged so that there are the minimum number of days with the full load falling on one of us alone.

CAROLINE Too damned often.

CHAIRMAN You think so, Mrs Smith.

CAROLINE I'm sure of it. And Robert knows it. They both spent half their lives running after people with a few spots or running noses looking for free pills.

CHAIRMAN The poor may be sick too, Mrs Smith.

CAROLINE And the middle-aged-class women with their piddling little worries, their veins and their over-filled bellies. That's what did for our marriage, you know. I couldn't stand the pace. The bloody telephone, the calls, the complaints and seeing him for breakfast and bed—breakfast and bed!

CHAIRMAN Thank you, Mrs Smith. I think you've explained how you feel fairly adequately.

Fade.

A telephone rings loudly and for some time.

SMITH Dr Smith.... Who? Oh, Brownlow.... Yes I know I haven't called yet.... Of course he's got a temperature—it's mumps. You'll get a visit after evening surgery.... Well I'm sorry. It's the earliest I can do for you today—it's been rather a busy day.... What's that? Oh I'm sure you've had a busy day too.... Well that's your prerogative. But if you do get another doctor, let me know—it will save me the trouble of calling tonight.

He puts the phone down—hard.

Cheeky bastard.

The door bell rings. He picks up the receiver.

(*into phone*) Dr Smith.... Who's that?

The door bell rings again.

Hell—it's the door.

He puts the phone down, goes to the hall and opens the door.

AILEEN Hello.

SMITH Hello.

AILEEN I had to come.

SMITH Anything wrong?

AILEEN No. I just couldn't settle.

SMITH Oh.

AILEEN I was worried about you.

SMITH Needn't have. I'm perfectly all right.

AILEEN I mean you woke up and went so quickly.... I started to worry.

SMITH No need. No need at all.

AILEEN I thought I'd find out.

SMITH Alice told you where I was I suppose.

AILEEN Yes.

SMITH Bus?

AILEEN No. I walked up the hill.... Are you going to ask me in?

SMITH Sorry. Of course.
She comes in and he shuts the door.
You worry too much.

AILEEN Can't help it.

SMITH I'll get Robert to put you on tranquillisers.

AILEEN I'd rather keep my worries, thank you.

SMITH If you want I'll give you a lift back. I'm off in five minutes.

AILEEN Have you had any tea?

SMITH All I want, thanks.

AILEEN I didn't ask that.

SMITH No.

AILEEN I'll make you some.

SMITH No! I don't want any bloody tea!
An awkward pause.
I'll get ready.... Go through and wait.

AILEEN I'm all right here.

SMITH Suit yourself. (*he goes off to wash*)

AILEEN Are these all Caroline's things?

SMITH (*loudly*) What?

AILEEN Are these Caroline's cases?

SMITH Yes. They're supposed to be coming for them tomorrow.

AILEEN (*reading a label*) Bishops Walk, Hertfordshire.

SMITH Her mother's place.

AILEEN I see.

SMITH What do you see?

AILEEN Nothing. It's just odd to find Caroline's cases when she's gone—for good.

SMITH It's worse upstairs! Wardrobe's empty. All her stuff out of the bathroom. Powder and make-up and things. Like a museum.

AILEEN You'll stay on here?

SMITH No. We're selling and splitting the proceeds between us. Fifty-fifty.

AILEEN Sounds so cold. Not even a big row to end with.

SMITH You don't shout when you're dead.... And we were dead for years.

AILEEN That's a funny thing to say—I mean Caroline's so lively.

SMITH And I'm not.

AILEEN I didn't say that.

SMITH No.... Coming then?

AILEEN David—why don't you take tonight off?

SMITH Night off? What for?

AILEEN Well, Caroline going and Elspeth dying and—

SMITH (*angry*) Don't be stupid.

AILEEN You could if you wanted. You've got an arrangement with Toby Day.

SMITH Don't interfere! There's no damn reason at all why I should drag Toby in. There's no emergency.

AILEEN Does it have to be an emergency?

SMITH It damn well does as far as I'm concerned. Now are you coming or not?

AILEEN Yes.... I could drive you if you like.

SMITH You could what?

AILEEN Drive you. Like I did the day you'd twisted your ankle.

SMITH (*angry*) When I want a wet nurse I'll tell you!

AILEEN If that's how you feel I'd rather walk, thanks.
She goes closing the door firmly behind her.

SMITH (*calls*) Aileen!... Oh hell!
Fade.

The tribunal.

CHAIRMAN Dr Smith was late for the evening surgery.

DAKERS Yes. Twenty minutes. He told his receptionist he'd had a sudden visit to make.

CHAIRMAN But we know he didn't.

DAKERS I'm afraid so.

CHAIRMAN So there were thirty minutes unaccounted for.

AILEEN He passed me on the hill.

CHAIRMAN He stopped perhaps after your quarrel, Miss Telford?

AILEEN Yes. To offer me a lift.

CHAIRMAN You accepted?

AILEEN No.

CHAIRMAN Why not?

AILEEN I disliked being shouted at. I told him I wasn't his wife.

CHAIRMAN So he shouted at his wife?

AILEEN I didn't say that.

CHAIRMAN But he did?

AILEEN Ask her—not me.

CHAIRMAN I will.

CAROLINE Yes. He shouted at me.

CHAIRMAN Often?

CAROLINE Enough.

CHAIRMAN You knew of this, Dr Tenniel?

TENNIEL Yes.

CHAIRMAN There were complaints from patients perhaps about this shouting, Dr Tenniel?

TENNIEL A few.... No more than I get myself.

CHAIRMAN That's something. But we still haven't solved the problem of the missing half hour, have we?... What about the surgery?

TENNIEL The surgery?

CHAIRMAN Yes. Were there any complaints?

TENNIEL None that I know of.

CHAIRMAN It was perfectly normal?

TENNIEL Not too big. There was a bit of trouble with an Irishman who'd cracked some ribs. (*he laughs*) And I understand he kept calling Mrs Jones, Mrs James.
Fade.

The noise of ash trays being emptied in bin.

ALICE Dirty beggars with their ash.

SMITH Now then, Alice—how many have you hidden behind your counter?

ALICE I'd like to hide some of them doctor.
Smith stumbles over a small table.
Steady! Are you all right, doctor?

SMITH Perfectly. Didn't see the damn table. You've had a long day, Alice—I thought Jenny took second surgery this week.

ALICE Baby's off colour. I told her not to bother.

SMITH Want me to call?

ALICE Don't you bother—just a few teeth coming through—and you've got your own calls.

SMITH The Raglan Terrace one?

ALICE That's it. Raglan Terrace. Oh! And you won't forget the Brownlows. He's been on the 'phone again—throwing his weight about a bit.

SMITH Thanks. I won't! Enjoy your weekend.

ALICE I will. Goodnight, doctor.

SMITH 'night, Alice.

Fade.

The tribunal.

CHAIRMAN And that—except for a handful of visits—was the end of Dr Smith's working day!

DAKERS Yes, Sir Joseph.

CHAIRMAN Long.

DAKERS Yes.

CHAIRMAN But not impossible.

DAKERS No.

CHAIRMAN A man worried by his domestic failure.

DAKERS Yes.

CHAIRMAN And unnecessarily weary through his own habit of pre-surgery visiting?

DAKERS Yes, Sir Joseph.

CHAIRMAN He made his evening visits—but he didn't go home as far as we know.

DAKERS No.

CHAIRMAN Another missing hour, Mr Dakers.

DAKERS I'm afraid so.

CHAIRMAN And he forgot one visit?

DAKERS Not quite, Sir Joseph.

CHAIRMAN No. You're right. He remembered—but only at the very end of his day—which was hardly calculated to please Mr Brownlow after all those telephone calls. How many were there? Four? Five?

Fade.

The sound of door chimes. A door opens and shuts.

SMITH Hello—doctor here—Anyone at home?

BROWNLOW (*angry*) About time, too. Gone nine.

SMITH Sorry. Busy day, Mr Brownlow.

BROWNLOW I've been ringing every half hour since lunch.

MRS BROWNLOW (*coming in*) John!

SMITH (*clearly amiable*) So they tell me.... Glad you can afford it. Evening, Mrs Brownlow.

BROWNLOW It's not bloody good enough, Smith.

MRS BROWNLOW Please, John.

SMITH It's the best you'll get, I'm afraid.

BROWNLOW Don't try to be clever with me. I help pay your wages. When I ask for a doctor on Thursday I expect to get him on Thursday—not last thing on Friday night, expecting everyone to bow down and kiss the ground in front of him.

SMITH (*still fairly amiable*) Mumps.

BROWNLOW Eh?

SMITH The lad's got mumps, not yellow fever. You don't need a doctor.

BROWNLOW And how the hell do you know? Telepathy?

BROWNLOW John! That's rude.

SMITH I saw the boy on Wednesday morning, Mr Brownlow. He had every symptom of incipient mumps.

BROWNLOW Marvellous. A three minute chat on your way to work and you have it all worked out. I think I'll...

SMITH (*loudly*) Now wait a minute. Wait one minute. I've just about had enough of this pantomime. You want me to see the boy?

BROWNLOW Oh yes, of course.

No answer from Brownlow.

SMITH Well, Mr Brownlow? Here. Take the tools. Do it yourself.... Or shut up and let me get on with my work. Or better still ring 4996 and they'll send an emergency doctor to do the job, and we'll all be happy.... Goodnight. (*going off*)

BROWNLOW Dr Smith.... Don't go. Please go up. Peter's in the back room.

SMITH (*sighs*) All right, Mrs Brownlow. (*he goes upstairs*)

BROWNLOW (*after a pause*) I'm ashamed of you, John. Carrying on like that.

BROWNLOW Don't interfere.

BROWNLOW You can see he's tired. He's been busy. He said so.

BROWNLOW We've all been busy. It's time they learned, they aren't God Almighty.

SMITH (*coming back*) Fortunately we don't have to be very often, Mr Brownlow.... Mumps. Not very bad. In a couple of days he'll be as right as rain. Sticking you for ice-cream and lemonade. Give him an aspirin in a warm milk drink before he goes to sleep.

BROWNLOW (*sneering*) Aspirin!

SMITH That's right. One aspirin.

BROWNLOW Well, it will make an appropriate end to my letter of complaint to the Medical Executive. Thirty-six hours waiting for a doctor—for an aspirin.

SMITH (*angry*) All right, Mr Brownlow, since that's the way you like it. Add a postscript—Dr Smith then turned me and my family off his list of patients.

BROWNLOW Oh-no-you-can't!

SMITH But I can! And I will! Tomorrow morning. I'll make a special journey to the surgery to put your cards in the post.

MRS BROWNLOW Oh, Dr Smith. Don't do that.

BROWNLOW He can't. He's just trying it on.

SMITH Sorry, Mrs Brownlow—for you, and Peter, but I don't see why we should put up with your pig of a husband any longer.

BROWNLOW Pig! Pig is it! By God I'll give you pig!

SMITH Don't be stupid.

He knocks over a vase which breaks.

MRS BROWNLOW My vase.

SMITH I'm sorry.

BROWNLOW *(triumphant)* I thought so. I've got you now. Pig am I? You stink of whisky. You're bloody drunk man!

SMITH Am I? Well how about this....

The sound of a blow followed by a body falling.
Brownlow groans.
Good night!
He bangs the door behind him.
Fade.

The tribunal.

CHAIRMAN Well, Mr Dakers?

DAKERS A most unfortunate set of circumstances. Dr Smith was badly provoked.

CHAIRMAN Nothing, Mr Dakers, nothing justifies violence on the part of a doctor.... And Brownlow was right. Dr Smith should have visited earlier.

DAKERS But Mr Brownlow's manner....

CHAIRMAN Was entirely consistent as an angry man, who felt he had a justifiable grievance. Dr Smith should have apologised, explained, seen the boy and left. His behaviour was appalling. And it was only the beginning of his disasters wasn't it?

DAKERS Yes, Sir Joseph, it was only the beginning.

Fade.

Sounds from the interior of a parked police car. Static crackle from radio.
Sounds of street traffic.

SERGEANT Right, Murphy. Nothing doing. Let's go.

MURPHY Yes, Serg.

The car starts.

SERGEANT Hold it.... What's this joker doing?

The sound of brakes. Sound of collision. Brakes squeal. Sound of another collision.

MURPHY He's going to pot the black one—when he's finished the reds.

SERGEANT The bloody fool's going to hit us.

A loud collision.

Pause.

MURPHY He did!

SERGEANT Come on.

The police leave the car, walk along the road and open Smith's car door. (*with obvious restraint*) Not very clever are we, Sir.

SMITH Sorry about that. I should have used a number eight iron.

MURPHY You all right, Sir?

SMITH Great. Never felt better.

SERGEANT Your head's cut.

SMITH Oh. Is it?

SERGEANT Could I see your driving licence, Sir?

SMITH Eh? Oh, yes. Here we are.

Murphy opens the rear door. There is the sound of disturbed bottles.

MURPHY Sergeant. . . . Take a look here.

Pause.

SERGEANT *Dr* Smith is it?

SMITH That's right.

SERGEANT Not been very sensible, have we, doctor?

SMITH Eh?

SERGEANT I mean this little lot.

SMITH Had to do something, sergeant—woman ran slap under my bonnet.

SERGEANT Not that, sir. . . . These. . . . You've been drinking, sir.

SMITH Can't deny that, sergeant.

SERGEANT More than the law permits if you're driving, doctor. . . . I shall have to ask you to do a test. Think you can stand all right?

SMITH (*laughs*) For God's sake, sergeant, you don't really think I'm drunk—do you?

Fade.

The tribunal.

CHAIRMAN But Dr Smith was drunk after all.

SERGEANT The magistrates said so. Blood test showed 200 m.g. per m.l. A very high figure indeed, sir.

CHAIRMAN But he was not drunk—in the normal sense of the word.

SERGEANT Far from it, Sir. Right as rain. Very friendly. Talked a bit too much maybe.

CHAIRMAN But. . . .

SERGEANT Alcoholic, sir. Probably been absorbing the stuff all day—and for months.

CHAIRMAN Guilty of course?

SERGEANT Of causing the accident? No, sir. Pedestrian admitted she'd run across the road. Dr Smith skidded on the wet surface.

CHAIRMAN But the other?

SERGEANT Too much alcohol in the blood? . . . Not a shadow of doubt, sir. Admitted it straight away of course. Very helpful he was. Fined fifty pounds, licence suspended for a year. Magistrates had no choice. . . . A bad job, Sir.

CHAIRMAN A bad job indeed. . . . Mrs Smith. Would you agree that Dr Smith was an alcoholic?

CAROLINE (*pause*) Yes—he had been one getting on for five years.

CHAIRMAN How bad?

CAROLINE Pretty bad at times.

CHAIRMAN It was this perhaps that broke up your marriage?

CAROLINE It was the final straw. Five years with a boozer was about as much as I could stomach.

CHAIRMAN I understand.

CAROLINE Nobody understands unless they've lived with one—and seen him go downhill. It's dirty and degrading and violent.

CHAIRMAN Violent?

CAROLINE Sometimes he would explode. . . .

CHAIRMAN He threw things?

CAROLINE From time to time. (*laughter*) He usually gave me time to duck.

CHAIRMAN Can you tell us why he drank?

CAROLINE I think so—we all have our dark corners. . . . He was working class. His patients were his own kind of people. He found it easy to understand them. I didn't want to. . . . I hated their whining and their scruffy diseases that littered our lives. I had money. He hadn't. I gave up a career in advertising for him. He had nothing to offer in exchange. Whatever we had was over almost before it began. We had nothing but sex—and that not for long. So he started to drink (*pause*) I don't think I helped him much in any way—I was pretty dejected and bitter about it all. . . . I hated him. . . . But not now. Now I feel nothing. Absolutely nothing. He's just a memory I lived through.

CHAIRMAN I see. Thank you. (*pause*) Dr Tenniel—I'm a little surprised that you didn't notice Dr Smith's drinking.

TENNIEL (*wary*) I knew he drank at parties—too much now and again— and I told him so. But never on duty. It would have showed and I assure you I would not have let it pass.

CHAIRMAN   Yet some of his patients guessed.

RS GORRINGE   Oh, I knew all right. Fair stank of whisky when he called to see me and the bairns.

MISS WARE   I call it a disgrace. Always drunk.

NDA DUNCAN   Not always. But he was stoned once or twice when he came.

BERT DYSON   Well they used to say as how 'e 'ad too much now and again but I never noticed it at six i' the morning like.

CHAIRMAN   I take it you were aware of this, Miss Telford?

AILEEN   Yes.

CHAIRMAN   On this particular day?

AILEEN   I offered to drive him.

CHAIRMAN   I remember. But you knew long before this I expect?

AILLEEN   Two years. Caroline warned me. He had accounts at two off-licences, used one and kept the other waiting a month for their money. Then he'd reverse the order for a month. He got two month's credit that way.

CHAIRMAN   He was in financial difficulties?

AILEEN   Not particularly. . . . Just short of cash for drinking.

CHAIRMAN   And how has it been since that day?

AILEEN   I haven't seen him or heard from him since. . . . And I don't want to until he's sober for good. . . . Then I'd like to marry him.

CHAIRMAN   I see. . . . Mr Dakers—have you anything else to say on Dr Smith's behalf?

DAKERS   No, Sir Joseph.

CHAIRMAN   Thank you. And I would like to thank all those who have given evidence in this sad and difficult enquiry. Two things I think require to be said:

First: Dr Smith is in many ways a very fine doctor, talented, and hard-working. One might almost use an overworked word and say devoted. In addition to his skill as a doctor, he possesses a rare understanding and sympathy for his fellow man. Whatever the outcome of this enquiry I would like him to know he has the committee's appreciation of his work.

Secondly: Mr Dakers has skilfully and patiently presented Dr Smith's plea that this was a long and exhausting day where medical and domestic problems forced Dr Smith beyond human endurance. But this is an argument that cannot be sustained. A doctor holds in his hands the lives and happiness of his patients —not just for this day—or that—but every day. When we ask him for an account of his stewardship he must be able to say— Take any day.

Pause.

Now before I adjourn to consider the outcome of this enquiry I have one last question for Mrs Smith—which she is entirely free not to answer if she wishes.

CAROLINE Yes?

CHAIRMAN Would you have been entirely happy to have had your husband attend your own children on that last day?

CAROLINE (*pauses—then quietly*) No.
A buzz of reaction.
Fade.

The sounds of a park. Children playing. Water lapping. Herbert Dyson wheezing and coughing.

DYSON Well, look who's 'ere.

SMITH Eh?

DYSON I said it's a lovely day, doctor.

SMITH Herbert! You old villain. I was sleeping off a big lunch. How are you?

DYSON Well as I'll ever be. Choking—inch by inch, like.

SMITH Looking after you are they?

DYSON Young fella Tenniel's got these days keeps pokin' different coloured pills down me gullet and I'm not dead yet. . . . Mollie died you know.

SMITH I heard. I'm sorry.

DYSON Old lass turned over and snuffed it. Just like that.

SMITH Stroke?

DYSON Aye. Didn't know you'd heard about that.

SMITH She had two little ones—five years ago Herbert. We didn't bother you with them. Thought it might get on your chest.

DYSON Oh. I see. . . . A bloody conspiracy. And 'ow are you, doctor?

SMITH Fine—but no doctor these days, Herbert.

DYSON That's a tale. You don't change folk by crossing them off a register.

SMITH I wonder.

DYSON Gone two year 'asn't it?

SMITH Three, Herbert.

DYSON You'll be staying maybe?

SMITH No.

DYSON Visiting folk like?

SMITH Working. Selling business equipment these days, Herbert. Modernising Britain.

DYSON Money all right?

SMITH Better than dishing out number nines to old frauds like you.

DYSON But not good enough to make thee forget it, eh?

SMITH Sometimes. It's not as hard as you'd think, Herbert. Not when you've had a real bellyful.

DYSON And t'other?

SMITH Booze? Dry as an old stick. . . . Dead men don't drink. And I'm dead.

DYSON No kidding.

SMITH No kidding. Not a drop.

DYSON Luv'ly, luv'ly. I knew you'd do it. You can ask for your ticket back? They said two years didn't they?

SMITH If I wanted. If I ask, that is.

DYSON You will, though?

SMITH Depends.

DYSON Oh aye—on her?

SMITH On her.

DYSON Not seen her since?

SMITH No.

DYSON Ah. I see.

SMITH I wrote her a letter.

DYSON Offering to wed 'er like?

SMITH Something like that.

DYSON Aye—it usually arouses their interest.
We hear light staccato footsteps approaching.
(*explodes into wheezes*) I'll leave thee to it then. I never wer much of a gooseberry.
Smith laughs.

SMITH All right, Herbert.

DYSON (*as he goes*) Good day then, doctor. 'ere's wishing thee luck.

SMITH Thanks Herbert. Look after yourself.

DYSON Aye. I'd be right glad to see thee one o' these mornings for a game.
Dyson wheezes away.
The woman's footsteps get very close and stop.
Pause.

AILEEN Hello, David.

SMITH Hello, Aileen. It's been a long time.
Fade out.

Questions for Discussion and Suggestions for Writing

(Suggestions for writing are marked with an asterisk.)

We Could Always Fit a Sidecar

*1   Imagine that Harry is describing his workmates and his work to a friend. What do you think he would say about them?

2   What does the shoe-shop scene on page 5 add to your knowledge of Harry's character? How important are the shoes?

3   Do you think Harry expected Thelma's announcement of their engagement? (p. 14) Or has he been forced reluctantly into the whole affair? If so, why doesn't he get out of it?

*Your answer could be in the form of Harry's thoughts as he sits in his room after the outing. What is he referring to when he says "Ruined..." (p. 15)? What might he be thinking when Thelma comes in? Notice how little he says to her. And where do you think he might be planning to go when Mrs Baynes catches him in the hall?

4   How could the actor playing Harry convey his inner thoughts when he is answering Thelma in this scene?

5   When Harry and Thelma are quarrelling, Thelma accuses Harry of never thinking about peoples' feelings—"All you think about is your things". Harry answers that Thelma treats *him* as a thing—"summat to show off to your friends and the neighbours" (p. 22).

Do you agree with their judgements of each other? Do you feel that either one deserves more sympathy than the other? If so, who, and why?

6   In what ways have Harry and Thelma changed when they meet again at the end of the play? Is the change convincing? Do you think they have a fair chance of a happy marriage now?

7   Jack Baynes says: "Harry's like all the rest of us if you ask me—all right if he's left alone." (p. 10).

Is this a fair description of most men? And do most women, like Mrs Baynes, have to do the pushing? Try to give examples from your own experience to support your opinion.

8   Read *The Human Element* by Stan Barstow (in the Longman

Imprint book of the same title). This is the short story on which the play is based.

Does the fact that the story is told in the first person change your feelings towards Harry?

Compare the endings. Which do you prefer, and why?

Is there anything else you feel differently about after reading the story?

Why do you think Stan Barstow changed the title?

There's No Point In Arguing the Toss

9   If you were producing the play, how would you ask the actor playing George to read his first speech? What sort of mood would you want to establish?

If you find this difficult to answer, ask someone to read the speech in as many different ways as they can and then try to work out which one sounds best, and why.

10   How does the writer manage to make the tragic subject of death so comic? Pick out some passages which you find especially funny. Try to say why.

Are there moments when you feel that the play is sad as well as funny?

11   In the notes on the authors (p. 148) Hallam Tennyson is quoted as saying that Don Haworth's characters "stand for integrity, for poetry, for a kind of divine and indestructible virtue".

Does this description fit Fred? What do you think Hallam Tennyson meant by "poetry"? In what ways does Fred show integrity?

12   How does the play treat figures of authority—the attendant at the Ghost Train, or the bus conductor? What do you notice about their language? Why do you think they react to the situation as they do?

13   On p. 39 Fred says, "We owe it to him to take him home in a normal decent manner on the bus." Obviously not everyone would agree that what they do is "normal and decent". What do you think?

14   Fred's feelings about his dad are complex. Try to sum them up in your own words. Why do you think the moment where he sat drinking tea with his dad after failing the eleven-plus meant such a lot to Fred?

15   "Passing on doesn't make him a saint" (p. 44).

Why do you think people often talk about the dead as if

they *were* saints?

* 16 Imagine a situation where *you* have to behave in an un-
conventional way—perhaps wearing something odd, or
travelling on public transport with some unusual luggage.
What happens? How do people react to you? (Maybe you
have a real experience to describe?)

Relics

17 Why do you think the writer introduces us first to the spirit
of Aunt Dorothy? What difference does it make to the way
you react to the main scene?

18 If you were producing this play, how would you make it
clear to the listeners that Aunt Dorothy is a ghost?

19 "One builds up a rampart of possessions against the time
when all else fails. All else has failed. But could they hold
one?...Can one not let go?" (p. 57).
What do you think Aunt Dorothy means by "all else"?
What comfort do you suppose her possessions gave her? And
why does she want to be able to let go? Why didn't she sell
the box?

20 Why doesn't Una want to be thought of as "rummaging"
(p. 59)?
Does she care about her dead aunt, or does she only care
about what other people might think? Look carefully at all
her speeches and give some examples to support your
opinion.

21 If you were producing this play, what kind of voices would
you choose for the three nieces, to help bring out the differences between their characters?

22 What does Olive mean when she says she had lost her
dignity for a while—"I'm trying to recover it" (p. 66)?
Does she recover it? What do you think Olive feels towards
her aunt?

23 "She had standards" (p. 63).
Try to describe the standards you think Aunt Dorothy had.
Do you admire them?

24 What do you understand by Aunt Dorothy's last words?
"All gone. Except...Adrian? Arthur? Ah!" (p. 69) And
what does her "long contented sigh" mean?

* 25 Write a short scene where one of the nieces returns home
and tells her husband about the visit to Aunt Dorothy's
house. What would she say about the other two nieces?

Jump!

26 "*Jump!* is a fable. Its apparent simplicity is deceptive and the story is capable of more than one interpretation" (Introduction, p. 73).

A fable is a story intended to teach a moral lesson. What moral lesson do you think *Jump!* teaches? Are you more, or less ready to learn the lesson if it is told in such a light-hearted way?

27 Why do you think Frederick and Mr Morrisarde believe the mole straight away, whereas everyone else doubts the story?

28 "Man's strongest faith is in his own capacity for disbelief" (p. 80). Can you think of any examples in the world today of humans refusing to believe something? What could convince them, do you suppose?

29 Why does Mr Morrisarde mention the fact that "man's laughter is spelled the same as manslaughter" (p. 86)? Does it have any connection with the main theme of the play?

30 Gumbolt, the White Master, accuses humans of doing their best to harm the world (p. 90). How many crimes can you think of that man has committed against the world?

31 What do you understand by "brinkmanship" (p. 91)? Can you think of an example of brinkmanship in international affairs?

*32 *Either*

Imagine you are a radio or newspaper reporter at the time of the Great Jump. Record or write an "on the spot" report —include a picture with the writing if you can.

Or

Describe how your family react to the instructions to jump. You could write this as a short play if you like.

*33 Try writing your own animal fable. You could use a proverb for the moral lesson (e.g. "A bad workman blames his tools" or "Pride goes before a fall") and then work out a story or play to illustrate it. It will need careful planning. Reading Aesop's Fables might help you.

Take Any Day

34 Two of Dr Smith's patients, Herbert Dyson and Dorothy Dinely, speak up for him at the tribunal. Dyson says that Dr Smith's company "did me a damn sight better than the

pills I'm tekkin'" (p. 115). Dorothy says she felt "almost elated" after Dr Smith told her about her illness (p. 115). Try to describe the qualities in Dr Smith that made him such a popular doctor.

35   The chairman feels that Dr Smith "interfered with things not really in his province" (p. 105). Do you agree with him? Try to explain what Dr Smith's reasons for interfering might have been.

36   Who would you prefer as your doctor, Tenniel or Smith? Why?

37   Is Aileen "a selfish bitch" (p. 119)? Or is Dr Smith impossible to live with?

38   Why do you think Dr Smith refuses to take the night off, or to accept any of the help Aileen offers? (pp. 122–4).

39   "Nothing justifies violence on the part of a doctor" (p. 128). Do you agree with the chairman? If so, how could the situation have been avoided?

40   At the end of the play, everything seems hopeful for the future. Will Aileen and David marry? Will it work? Will he "ask for his ticket back" as a doctor? Do you think he should? How do you think Aileen might succeed as a doctor's wife where Caroline failed?

  *You could answer these questions in the form of a short sequel to the play—a scene set a year or two later.

General

41   "Unlike the novelist, the radio writer cannot describe the appearance of his characters except through the words they address to one another." (*Writing For Radio*, p. 153.).
Choose any *two* characters from the plays, and describe how you visualise their physical appearance. What clues did you use to arrive at that particular picture in your imagination?

42   "The producer has just four ingredients: voices, sounds, music, and (very important) silence." (*Producing Radio Plays in Schools*, p. 140.)
Find two or three places in any of the plays where you would use *silence* as an important ingredient. What would you want the silence to convey in each case?

*43   "The dialogue has to do several things simultaneously; it must create character. . .it has to carry the action forward . . .it must reveal information in a way which appears natural. . . . Above all dialogue must have vitality and spontaneity." (*Writing for Radio*, p. 153.)

Choose one scene from any of the plays which seems to you to achieve all the aims mentioned in the above passage. Look at it in detail and explain carefully why you have chosen that particular scene.

Producing Radio Plays in Schools

Michael Marland and Alfred Bradley

The core of a radio play, like that of any other form of drama, is the meeting of characters and the clashes of ideas and temperaments that follow: Harry and Thelma, Una and Winifred, Fred and the bus conductor, etc. But a radio play is an invention in sound only, and the conflict, the characters, the ideas, the fun, and the tensions have to be put over by means of a loudspeaker—and nothing else. The producer has just four ingredients: voices, sounds, music and (very important) silence. He must calculate, organise and control these four ingredients very carefully indeed so that he makes the best use of them. The sounds that we hear in real life are often blurred when transmitted through a microphone and loudspeaker: anybody who has tried to record the witty conversation and atmosphere of a party will know that the result is likely to be a muddy and incomprehensible noise. A radio production must impose a discipline on the different elements bringing out only the sounds or voices which have importance at a particular moment.

You probably know something of the equipment used by the BBC to help the producer control these sounds: studios specially treated to provide contrasting acoustics, separate glass-windowed control room, numerous microphones, mixers, echo chambers, etc. Is there any hope, then, of making even a reasonable shot at producing these plays with the makeshift equipment of a school and a cast of pupil actors? A very few new schools are being built with modestly but efficiently equipped recording studios. What of the rest? It is difficult, and results will certainly be less than perfectly polished, but effective productions can be done. It is worth remembering that much of the professional equipment is designed and installed simply to save *time*, for staff is limited and expensive and a professional broadcasting organisation has to put out a large number of productions. Given time, patience and ingenuity similar results can often be achieved on more modest equipment. Full details of equipment, the operation of tape-recorders and recording techniques suitable for schools will be found in the books listed below. This note will discuss the application of these to the effective recorded production of the five plays.

COLLISON, DAVID, *Stage Sound*, Studio Vista

JONES, GRAHAM J, *Teaching with Tape*, Focal Press

MALLORY, L, *The Right Way to Tape Record*, Eliot *Right Way* Books, (Easy to use)

METHOLD, KENNETH, *Broadcasting with Children*, U L P

NISBETT, ALEC, *The Technique of the Sound Studio*, Focal Press

WOODMAN, H, *The Drama Tape Guide*, Focal Press

NATIONAL FOUNDATION FOR VISUAL AIDS, *The Tape Recorder in the Classroom* (Particularly good on the machine itself)

Equipment

Almost any tape recorder can be used (for fuller information see *Teaching with Tape*), but for reasonable results a suitable microphone should be added. This is a ribbon microphone which picks up sound from two directions only. An omni-directional microphone is not suitable for dramatic work—it does not *select* the sounds that are wanted.

The essence of recording a play is control of the sound, *knowing* what is being recorded. The second technical requirement, therefore, is some means of 'monitoring', or listening to the recording *as it is being made*. The simplest way of doing this is to buy a pair of headphones so that the 'recording engineer' or 'studio manager' can listen to what is going on to the tape, and adjust the volume according to his judgement.

The best way is to arrange the microphones and performers in one room and have long leads to the producer and engineers in a separate sound-proof 'control' room. This allows the monitoring to be done through a loudspeaker and to be heard by a group of people. For ease of operation and really effective production, a 'talk-back' system is required, so that by flicking a switch the producer in the control room can be heard by the performers. He can in this way advise the performers in rehearsal and between sections of the recording. Ideally there should be a window through which he can be seen, and cue-lights are helpful so that he can give precise signals to performers. Some schools have converted store-rooms, cupboards, or adjoining classrooms as control rooms; others have built small $(6' \times 6' \times 6')$ 'rooms' out of a double layer of hardboard with fibre-glass as sound insulation. A control room like this can be set up in a corner of the school hall. A temporary but less satisfactory arrangement is to draw the stage curtains, using the stage as a 'control room' and the hall as a 'studio'.

The third technical requirement is the ability to 'mix' the various sounds so that, in the Town Hall in *Jump!*, for instance, the volume of the fanfares, crowd scenes and that of the actors' voices can be carefully controlled. The easiest way, of course, is to play the fanfare on a record player in the studio, picking the sound up on the actors' microphone, and using the record-player's own volume control to get the levels right. The best way, however, is to connect a *mixer-unit* to the tape-recorder which is being used for recording the play. It is then possible to plug the microphone, a record-player, and other tape-recorders or record-players into the mixer. Each *sound source* can have a separate volume control on the mixer and the exact balance of sounds can be chosen. In the scene in *We Could Always Fit a Sidecar* where Mrs Baynes and Thelma are preparing dinner, for instance, the test match commentary (previously recorded) might be played on tape, the crockery effects might be on one microphone and the actors on another. The engineers can then *mix* the sounds at the right levels.

The acting

A real advantage of sound drama for schools is that the ability to project the voice to the back of the hall that is required for stage productions is not necessary. It is important, though, to choose actors for what their *voices* suggest, not for what they look like. This is best done by auditioning through the monitor loudspeaker, judging suitability by ear alone. Each play requires contrasting voices, and each character requires a voice of the right pitch, quality and atmosphere. What differences, for instance, should there be between Frederick's Uncle and Professor Morrisarde in *Jump!*, the three nieces in *Relics*, or between Harry and the first Mechanic in *We Could Always Fit a Sidecar*? Rehearsals are usually best started sitting round a table away from the microphone. The actors need to concentrate first on *clarity*. With only the words to convey meaning, a radio production must above all be clear. They should then consider the *expression*. Think about the characters in *Relics*. A simple example is Winifred's remark after Mrs Parkinson leaves. *Una, drop the catch on that front door, after her.* How should this be said? Sometimes the things said between the lines are important. When

Aileen and David argue after she comes to see him we must realise that they still care for each other. Although David is in a tense mood he must retain our sympathy or we will cease to care about him and lose interest in the play.

Pauses are most important. When Harry meets Thelma at the end of *We Could Always Fit a Sidecar*, for instance, he tries to cover his embarrassment by talking about trivialities: *Is this my clean washing?* For the rest of the scene, until he tells her that he is sorry that they parted, there are a number of places where pauses will point to the fact that the couple want to talk to each other but don't know how to break the ice.

As rehearsals progress, the actors will practise and learn all these points, as well as their positions in relation to the microphone (which will be discussed next). Radio acting is usually best with the actors *standing*, and using facial expressions and even some movement of the body to help their voices. They should take great care when turning the pages of copies, as the rustling of paper is easily picked up by the microphone. An obtrusive script noise gives the listener an unpleasant jolt just as a loud prompt breaks the illusion in the theatre.

Space in sound

The listener will hear all the sounds and all the voices from one point: the loudspeaker. But the listener can be given a sense of space, particularly of the positions of the characters, by how the actors are positioned during the recording, and how they speak to the microphone. This is called the *aural perspective* of the recording. The microphone represents the listener, and in any scene the producer needs to decide where the listener is imagined to be. The actors should then be close or distant to the microphone according to the layout of the imagined scene. In the tribunal scenes in *Take Any Day*, for instance, the listener could be imagined to be behind the bench: the chairman will therefore be near the microphone, and the witnesses heard from further away. It will help if the scene can be recorded in a gymnasium or other large room and if the witnesses pitch up their voices it will not only suggest that they are speaking from a distance but will help to bring out the lively accoustic which suggests the atmosphere of a courtroom. Similarly, in the scene where Harry is cleaning his motor bike in *We Could Always Fit a Sidecar*, Thelma would be heard approaching the microphone, but her voice would never be quite as close as Harry's. (A small room where the hard plaster wall surfaces can be muffled with curtains, blankets or fibre-glass insulation would help to 'deaden' the atmosphere and would also be useful for the picnic scenes and the outdoor sequences in *Jump!*)

Perspectives should be decided by the producer and are most important. In particular, he must be consistent within one scene so that the listener is not confused. However, there is nothing very difficult or complicated about arranging them. If, as is best, a ribbon microphone is being used, giving two *live* sides and two *dead* sides distance can be achieved by simply moving round from the *live* to the *dead* side. The approaching Mrs Parkinson in *Relics*, for instance, starts talking on the *dead* side, and gradually moves round.

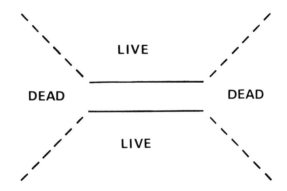

Sound effects

1 *Spot effects* are made in the studio by the Studio Managers and recorded at the same time as the actors: footsteps, the splintering of the box in *Relics*, the sounds of Harry climbing the ladder in *We Could Always Fit a Sidecar*. Doors are important as they indicate that somebody is entering or leaving a room. A wooden door-box fitted with a variety of locks and latches can suggest a front or back door, or with a suitable chime added, a shop door. A small box fitted with a number of contrasting bells and buzzers is another useful accessory as it enables sounds to be placed where they match the position of the actor when he is ringing a doorbell or answering the telephone.

2 *Effects records* can be bought (from EMI or BBC Records, London SE99) and provide a good range of standard sounds such

as the country backgrounds in *Jump!* or the car crashes in *Take Any Day*.

3 *Special recordings* can easily be made, particularly with a portable battery recorder, and it would be necessary for the background in the workshop in *We Could Always Fit a Sidecar*, the bus terminus in *There's No Point in Arguing the Toss* and probably the hymn singing as well.

In some of these plays, music is important in suggesting a scene and it should not be difficult to choose appropriate music for the restaurant in *Take Any Day* and the fairground music at the start of *There's No Point in Arguing the Toss*. When the brass band recordings were made for the BBC production of *Jump!* the opportunity was taken to record some extra incidental music which was used to provide background atmosphere when the mole described the landscape and, in a different mood, to suggest the tension Frederick felt as he climbed the crag. Although the producer should always be on the lookout for opportunities to use music to add to the mood, bridge scenes, or heighten the suspense in a play, he must resist the temptation to use music where it may only be a distraction.

Putting the play together

Each play has an overall shape and rhythm which depends on the speed of the acting in each scene, the way each starts and ends, and the sound or silence between scenes. It is easier to record the play scene by scene, or at least in groups of scenes. These sections can then be played back, and re-recorded if necessary. It is, of course, very easy to *cut* the tape and re-join it. This makes it possible to record some scenes twice, and later to cut out the least good. It also makes it possible to alter the length of the gap between scenes after the whole play has been recorded.

The fades that start and end most scenes are of great importance. The effect of fading-in suggests that life has been going on before the scene starts and that the listener is, as it were, dropping in. The fade needs to be gradual—not so slow that it gives a misleading air of mystery, and not so quick that it jerks with an over-dramatic emphasis. Where there are background noises that start the scene and are heard throughout, it is effective to fade up the background quite high to establish it, and then to fade it down and hold it under the dialogue of the scene.

Drama in sound

These five plays were invented in their writers' minds as dramas in sound. It was radio that first brought them to life. Each has a quality that is *aural* and not *visual*. The narrator's comments in *There's No Point in Arguing the Toss*, for instance; the thoughts which run through Harry's mind in *We Could Always Fit a Sidecar*; the conversations between Frederick and the mole in *Jump!*. All these are creations that can excite the imagination of listeners—even on a modest school tape-recorder.

This essay is reproduced (in slightly adapted form) from an article entitled *Producing Sound Drama in Schools* by Michael Marland in *Worth a Hearing*, a collection of radio plays compiled by Alfred Bradley published by Blackie and Son Limited.

The Authors

Stan Barstow

Stan Barstow was born in Yorkshire in 1928. He is married, with a son and a daughter, and worked in the engineering industry until the success of his first novel, *A Kind of Loving*, and the film subsequently made from it, enabled him to become a full-time writer in 1962.

His work for the theatre includes *Listen for the Trains, Love*, an adaptation of Ibsen's *An Enemy of the People*, and collaborations with Alfred Bradley on *Stringer's Last Stand* (Samuel French, 1972), and adaptations of his novels *Ask Me Tomorrow* (Samuel French, 1966) and *A Kind of Loving* (Blackie, 1970).

The Royal Television Society gave Stan Barstow its 1975 Writer's Award for his dramatisations of *A Raging Calm*, *Joby*, and Winifred Holtby's *South Riding*—the latter also receiving the Writers' Guild of Great Britain Best Television Dramatisation Award for 1974.

Stan Barstow's books, published by Michael Joseph, and also available in Corgi paperback editions, are the novels *A Kind of Loving* (1960), *Ask Me Tomorrow* (1962), *Joby* (1964), *The Watchers on the Shore* (1966), *A Raging Calm* (1968), and two volumes of short stories, *The Desperadoes* (1961) and *A Season with Eros* (1971). His latest novel, *The Right True End*, completes the trilogy begun with *A Kind of Loving* and continued in *The Watchers on the Shore*.

Two collections of his short stories are available in this series: *A Casual Acquaintance and other stories* and *The Human Element and other stories*. The author has recorded four of the stories himself to accompany the volumes: *Holroyd's Last Stand* and *A Casual Acquaintance* (Longman C.60 Compact Cassette 0 582 24079 4) and *One of the Virtues* and *The Human Element* (Longman C.60 Compact Cassette 0 582 24083 2).

We Could Always Fit a Sidecar, based on his short story *The Human Element*, was voted the Best Radio Drama Script of 1974 by the Writers' Guild.

The Cost of Loving was televised by ITV in 1977.

Don Haworth

Don Haworth was born at Bacup in Lancashire and educated at Burnley Grammar School. He served on flying duties in the Royal Air Force and worked in several parts of the world as a journalist before joining the BBC. He worked for Television News, the original Tonight, and Panorama and is now a documentary film producer for the BBC based at Manchester.

His plays have been broadcast in thirty-five countries. Six of them, *We All Come To It in the End*, *There's no Point in Arguing the Toss*, *The Prisoner*, *Where is this here Building—by what Route do I get there?*, *The Illumination of Mr Shannon* and *The Enlightenment of the Strawberry Gardener* were published in 1972 by BBC Publications under the title *We All Come To It in the End*. His earlier plays were: *The Man with the Red Door*, *A Time in Cloud Cuckoo Land* and *Simcocks Abound Across the Earth*. Since the publication of the collection he has written six more: *The Eventful Deaths of Mr Fruin*, *A Damsel and Also a Rough Bird*, *Mr Bruin Who Once Drove the Bus*, *Events at the Salamander Hotel*, *On a Day in Summer in a Garden* and *Fun Balloons*.

Almost the whole of Don Haworth's writing is directed to radio. He has written only one play for the theatre, *A Hearts and Minds Job*, but several of the radio plays have been adapted and performed on the stage. *The Illumination of Mr Shannon* was performed on BBC Television and *The Prisoner* was adapted by the author and produced by Thames Television under the title *A Brisk Dip Sagaciously Considered*. *A Time in Cloud Cuckoo Land* was produced by Bayerische Rundfunk for German Television under the title *Ein Haus voll Zeit*.

The leading characters in the plays are often young people. *Mr Bruin Who Once Drove the Bus* was written specially for BBC Radio for Schools and published in Writing and Listening. Of the people in the plays Hallam Tennyson, of BBC Radio Drama, wrote: "Haworth's protagonists take on the dimensions of folk heroes without being sentimentalised or softened; the almost moronic innocence with which they cling to their ideals would probably madden us in real life as much as it maddens their fictional tormentors. And yet they stand for integrity, for poetry, for a kind of divine and indestructible virtue."

Don Haworth's first play *The Man with the Red Door* made no impression. His second, *There's No Point in Arguing the Toss*, written in two days, attracted keen critical attention, was broadcast three times within six months and chosen by the BBC for the Italia Prize. The play was produced at Leeds by Alan Ayckbourn and first broadcast on the Third Programme in April 1967.

David Campton

David Campton was born in Leicester, where he still lives, in 1924. When he left school at seventeen he worked as a clerk with the Leicester Education Authority and after spending three years as a flight mechanic in the Royal Air Force during the war returned to a similar desk job with the East Midlands Gas Board. In 1956, after having had some success as an amateur (*Sunshine on the Righteous* won the Leicestershire British Drama League Festival in 1954 and *The Laboratory* won first prize in an international competition organised by the Tavistock Repertory Company in London in 1956) he decided to sink or swim as a full-time writer.

He joined Associated Rediffusion where he worked as a script-writer on a number of television comedy series and later became a member of Stephen Joseph's Theatre in the Round company which presented plays in a room above the public library in Scarborough. Stephen Joseph, an exceptionally gifted producer, probably directed more new plays than anybody else at that time and, under his influence, David Campton wrote a play each season for the company to perform.

His plays for the theatre include *Out of the Frying Pan* (included in *New Directions* published by Hutchinson), *Soldier from the Wars Returning*, *Memento Mori*, *A Smell of Burning* and *Then...* (included in *Worth a Hearing*, Blackie's *Student Drama* series), a selection of short plays *Laughter and Fear* (Blackie's *Student Drama* series) and *Alison* (included in *Breaking Away* in this series).

Relics was originally produced for radio by Anthony Cornish at the BBC drama studio in Birmingham in 1974. Since then it has been adapted for the theatre and is available in an acting edition from Evans Plays.

Ken Whitmore

Ken Whitmore was born in December 1937 in Hanley in the Potteries and worked as a journalist until awarding himself a sabbatical year in 1973 to see if he could write without the stimulus of a newspaper deadline. He threw up his job, sold his home and dragged his wife, three children and dog to the heights of the countryside. The family cheerfully accepted the challenge of moving, first to Yorkshire and then to Cumbria, and were rewarded when the first short story he wrote was awarded the adult prize in *The Times Jonathan Cape* children's story competition *Times Anthology of Children's Stories*, published by Jonathan Cape.

After his first radio play *Haywire at Humbleford Flag* was accepted by the BBC he went on to write *One of Our Commuters is Missing* and *Jump!* which proved so successful that a stage version was commissioned by the Unicorn Theatre for Young People and presented at the Arts Theatre, London, in May 1976. Since then he has completed four more plays for radio. *The Caucasian in the Woodpile*, *The Story of a Penny Suit*, *Colder Than of Late*, and *Out for the Count*.

Jump! was written in Hebden in Wharfdale in 1974. The scar, the beck, the violets, Scar Top Cottage, the curlews, the moles and the cuckoo can all be found there.

Ivor Wilson

Ivor Wilson was born south of the Humber in 1924. He is married, with a son and a daughter and lives in Hull. At school he showed no great academic distinction but a fair talent for athletics and association football, which was carried over into teacher training in Sheffield.

In 1943 the war caught up with him, he joined the Fleet Air Arm and was posted to Canada. On returning to England his career almost came to an end when he inadvertently flew a Corsair fighter aircraft into the ground, causing, he says, considerable damage to the ground. Two years, nine months and thirty plastic surgery operations later it was clear that athletics and association football were out of the question so he returned to the academic fold as a teacher. He taught in a secondary modern school in Hull for the next fourteen years before moving into further education, teaching economics and politics.

Between 1962 and 1965 he wrote four thrillers: *But Not For Love*, *That Feeds on Men*, *Lilies that Fester* and *Empty Tigers* (all published by Collins) and began to write for radio in 1969. Since having his first play accepted, he has written twenty others which have gained a wide audience in Europe and the Commonwealth. He has contributed to the Radio 3 new writing programme *The Northern Drift*, has written a number of short stories, a one-act play *Trial and Error* (Sixth Windmill Series published by Heinemann) and, at present, is working on a full-length comedy for the theatre.

Take Any Day is Ivor Wilson's first radio play. In this study of a doctor suffering from the pressures of modern life he draws on experience gained during his long stay in hospital.

Useful Books

BBC Publications, 35 Marylebone High Street, London W1
Writing for the BBC

BBC Publications, *New Radio Drama*
BBC Publications, GILES COOPER: *Six Plays for Radio*
BBC Publications, HENRY REED: *Radio Plays*
BBC Publications, DON HAWORTH: *Radio Plays*
Blackie and Son, *Worth a Hearing: Five Radio Plays*
Penguin, *New English Dramatists Volume 12*
Faber, DONALD MCWHINNIE, *The Art of Radio*

Writing for Radio

The radio writer's main concern is not with sound effects but with dialogue. He has no scenery, costume or lighting to help in creating an atmosphere and, unlike the novelist, he cannot describe the appearance of his characters except through the words which they address to one another. The dialogue has to do several things simultaneously; it must create character—in a well written play each person should have a distinctive way of talking and we ought to be able to guess who is speaking without referring to the names printed in the margin; it has to carry the action forward or we will be left with a group of interesting and convincing characters without a story; it must reveal information in a way which appears natural—we have all heard dialogue where the writer has tried to cram too much information into a short space and come up with a clumsy phrase like "the gun I am holding in my left hand is loaded". Above all dialogue must have vitality and spontaneity; conversation which may be passable in real life can sound threadbare and lifeless on radio. Whatever brilliance a director may be able to bring to a script, no amount of embroidery or elaborate sound effect sequences will be able to disguise the fact that a play lacks substance or than an author has not considered his characters in depth.

If you decide to try your hand at writing a play, remember that well-drawn characters and good situations are more important than sound effects, and that a story based on a visit to the doctor, an interview for a job, a clash of personalities on the football field, or a problem that you have faced at home or at school will probably work out better than a "whodunnit?" or anything else which you have not experienced at first hand.